SECOND EDITION

IMPROVING
Classroom
Questions

Kenneth R. Chuska

D1036554

Phi Delta Kappa Educational Foundation
Bloomington, Indiana U.S.A.

WEST GEORGIA REGIONAL LIBRARY SYSTEM
Neva Lomason Memorial Library

Cover design by
Victoria Voelker

Cover photographs by
Vladimir Bektesh

Cover Model:
Alexander J. Walling
Ages 8 and 15

Phi Delta Kappa Educational Foundation
408 North Union Street
Post Office Box 789
Bloomington, IN 47402-0789
U.S.A.

Printed in the United States of America

Library of Congress Control Number 2003112257
ISBN 0-87367-849-4
Copyright © 2003 by Kenneth R. Chuska
Bloomington, Indiana

TABLE OF CONTENTS

INTRODUCTION

All learning begins with questions. Questions cause interactions: thought, activity, conversation, or debate. The character of a question shapes the quality and dynamics of the interaction. The skillful use of questions can lead students to become more actively involved in a lesson. Skillful questioning also can lead to more interaction among students and more student-initiated questions.

Questions are fundamental to teaching because they encompass the three central components of effective teaching: They provide information; they help students connect that knowledge to previous and subsequent learning; and they take students to the highest levels of learning, in which they apply knowledge in various situations in their lives. The attention teachers give to planning questions will determine how well they and the students achieve their educational goals.

Skillful questioning can lead students to do more higher-level thinking. Good questions can help both the teacher and the students focus on concepts, generalizations, laws, and principles, rather than on low-level objectives and outcomes.

However, for teachers to improve their questioning skills, they need to re-examine their views on educational practices, specifically their goals and objectives, curricula, textbook selection, perceptions of students' and teachers' roles, and student-assessment techniques.

For example, to make the best use of questions, the teaching plan must accentuate opportunities for student involvement. Thus questions should allow students some autonomy in the planning and processes of learning. Assessments must ask students to demonstrate what they have learned, not just simply to display their ability to memorize. The written curriculum must promote the investigation and application necessary for high-level learning.

The time invested in planning effective questions to meet classroom objectives will be worthwhile if it: 1) focuses on essential learning, 2) helps students add to their knowledge and transfer it to other subjects, 3) motivates students to take a real interest in the material, and 4) helps students apply essential learning to real problems, issues, and decisions.

The first chapter, "Why Ask Better Questions?" provides background on past efforts to improve teachers' questioning skills. It also examines four cultural trends influencing the importance of more effective questioning: 1) changes in the associations among school, work, and society; 2) the current explosion of knowledge; 3) the growing scarcity of quality teaching materials; and 4) the current emphasis on career preparation.

Chapter Two, "Questions as Motivators," presents strategies to promote student involvement and to solve the dilemma of trying both to cover required material and to find time for effective questioning. That chapter also discusses the effects of these strategies on students' performance on standardized tests.

Chapter Three, "Designing Questions," explains the importance of using different questioning methods to pursue short- and long-term objectives. It also examines how questions should be used before, during, and after a unit of work to achieve different purposes.

The fourth chapter, "Specific Questioning Strategies," includes examples from the author's workshops and courses in thinking and questioning skills to illustrate questioning strategies that may be applied to elementary, secondary, and college levels. It also describes some successful, commercial programs on questioning strategies.

Chapter Five, "Shaping the Question-Response Transaction," presents strategies to anticipate students' responses. It examines students' roles in the question-response transaction, the factors that motivate them to respond, and the factors that influence the nature of their responses.

The sixth chapter, "Improving Assessment, Evaluation, and Testing with Better Questioning," stresses the importance of preparing students for formal testing. The use of skillful questioning needs to be emphasized equally both in evaluations and in the classroom. This chapter suggests strategies to encourage students to succeed in and to learn from tests.

Chapter Seven, "Asking Effective Questions Automatically," provides a plan for effective questioning that is designed for increasing competency levels. The more individual the plan, the more successful it will be. This chapter equips teachers with questioning strategies that will make students think and use their knowledge. These strategies will help teachers learn more about their students and discover more enjoyment in being a teacher.

For this second edition, I have added new material to some chapters and several appendices. The appendices include checklists for teachers and students on what makes a good question (Appendix 1) and tips for creating written tests (Appendices 2 and 3). Appendix 4 provides useful test-taking strategies for students. Appendix 5 suggests some points to ponder when evaluating student responses. The two final appendices provide a classroom observation protocol (Appendix 6) and a key to analyzing it (Appendix 7), which may be particularly helpful in self-analysis or teacher mentoring situations.

CHAPTER ONE

Why Ask Better Questions?

An apt way to begin a book about questioning might be to ask some questions of you, the reader. Consider: What would make a student look forward to attending your class? What would motivate a student to get involved in your lesson? What would excite a student about learning? What would evoke student curiosity?

My answer is, improved questioning.

Much has been written about improving teachers' questioning skills. In his landmark work, *Children's Thinking* (1956), David Russell argues that questions can be used to stimulate creative thought and lead to ideas, processes, and solutions that enhance the quality of life. He argues that the skillful use of questions will ensure that students accumulate adequate knowledge for critical thinking and will increase students' ability to see relationships. In addition, it will teach students to use questioning to solve other problems and to approach a problem differently.

Benjamin Bloom's work, *Taxonomy of Educational Objectives: Handbook 1: Cognitive Domain*, also was published in 1956. Bloom lists six levels of thinking to be addressed by appropriate questioning: knowledge, comprehension, application, analysis, synthesis, and evaluation. Since then, much teacher staff-development time has been devoted to interpreting Bloom's work. Although Bloom intended the *Taxonomy* to be a diagnostic tool, it often has been treated as if it were a prescriptive work. Thus teachers typically have been asked to evaluate their questioning strategies by using the *Taxonomy* as a yardstick, and the formulation of questions to fit the various domains was stressed in the hope that thinking levels would match questioning levels.

Norris M. Sanders' *Classroom Questions: What Kinds?* (1966) applied the *Taxonomy* to improving questioning in the social sciences. Sanders provides a method for teachers to lead students through a series of questioning levels in order to promote higher-level thinking and to reduce questions that emphasize memory and recall.

In *Teaching Strategies and Cognitive Functioning in Elementary School Children* (1966), Hilda Taba, another leader in improving teachers' questioning skills, argues that instructional strategies should follow a developmental sequence to enable students' cognitive functioning to exceed what typically is expected of them. In her work with the Contra Costa Schools in California, Taba carried out her three-level cognitive mapping approach to questioning: 1) concept development, which emphasizes the equal importance of attention to content and learning how to apply content; 2) the interpretation of data, which involves analyzing cause and effect; and 3) the application of generalizations, which calls for extending generalizations, identifying trends, and making predictions. Taba's premise is that teachers should not supply what students must develop by themselves.

Thomas Gordon introduced the concept of "active listening" in *Teacher Effectiveness Training* (1974). Gordon stresses the need to use active listening skills during questioning to encourage reflective thinking. Active listening can make students feel that their ideas and feelings are understood and respected. It includes such skills as clarifying a student's response by restating it, giving undivided attention to students while they respond, and developing an open and humane learning atmosphere.

Many of these authors focus on how *teachers* should improve their questioning skills. Francis P. Hunkins (1976) adds another dimension by emphasizing the value of helping students develop their own questioning skills. Hunkins stresses that the role of the student must be active, not passive. Teachers should strive to be designers and facilitators of learning situations, thus enabling students to become processors, rather than simply reproducers, of information. He advocates that students use questioning techniques such as those used by scholars and professionals.

J.T. Dillon (1988) also proposes that the teacher's role be the model for student involvement in questioning. He classifies the types of questions students ask in the classroom as: procedural (asking for instructions), conversational (asking the teacher to repeat information), self-answered, and rhetorical. Dillon also analyzes the three stages of classroom questioning: teachers' questions, students' responses, and teachers' reactions to those responses. Earlier writers also supported the interactive roles and responsibilities of teacher and student in the question-response transaction. Annamarie Palincsar (Palincsar and Brown 1985) furthered the idea of student involvement through a method, Reciprocal Teaching, that emphasized the interactive roles and responsibilities of both the teacher and student in the questioning and answering process. Her method is described in Chapter Four.

Trends Affecting Education

Four cultural trends are primarily responsible for renewed attention to questioning in the classroom: 1) changes in the associations among school, work, and society; 2) the current explosion of knowledge; 3) the dumbing down of basic teaching materials; and 4) the increased attention to preparing students for work and for continued education. One example of this atmosphere of change is the 1983 document, *A Nation at Risk*, which recommended a renewed emphasis on higher-level thinking skills in schools.

Bringing Life to the Classroom. As people change, their needs change. They need to acquire new skills or to consider new ideas. Thus students not only need to learn, they need to learn how to learn. Bruner (1966) stresses that students should be aware of the questioning process in order to learn how to learn.

In school, however, texts often merely summarize all that went into resolving a problem, decision, or issue, creating little opportunity for exploration and questioning. The challenge for teachers is to analyze the content of texts, which mainly include just facts, and to transform that information into situations that are based on problems, issues, decisions, and interests.

Equipping students with knowledge they can apply outside of school also requires promoting their autonomy in the classroom. This means that the questioning skills of both teachers and students need to be improved. If students have some control over their learning, they will be more likely to learn for themselves, rather than just for the teacher. Just as writing improves writing skills and reading improves reading skills, so practicing questioning will increase students' questioning skills.

Questioning also should help students identify similar processes to use in solving other problems in school and in their lives. For example, the student, while learning about a particular place, also should learn how to learn about anything identified as a place. The study of any place involves a similar process. Questioning must equally emphasize the topic and the process of learning about any similar topic. Thus questioning must enable students to apply their learning about a particular place to any other place.

The Knowledge Explosion and Its Fallout. We live in an information age. The most explosive aspect of this information age is the Internet. It is estimated that there are up to 2 billion publicly accessible pages on the World Wide Web. These pages present information on almost everything imaginable, available to any person with the technology and notion to go searching for it. In 1995, when this book was first released, there were an estimated 26 million people on the Web, today there are approximately 600 million people accessing the information highway.

How can anyone possibly keep up?

A byproduct of the explosion of knowledge is an explosion of ignorance. As this text is read, people will be born, ideas will be generated, technology will be developed, products will enter the market, and life-enhancing processes will be developed; and no individual can be aware of all of them.

Curricula and texts cannot possibly keep up with the flow of information. When devising classroom questions, teachers must take this explosion of knowledge (and ignorance) into account. Teachers should analyze the massive amount of information to determine how it can be reduced, integrated, or eliminated in order to best use classroom time.

The maxim should be "less *allows for* more." By asking fewer questions that focus on facts, data, and raw information, teachers allow more time for high-level questions that require student involvement in the answers. Thus teachers will increase student involvement and interactive learning, as opposed to creating isolated learning conditions. Teachers then can focus on concepts, generalizations, and laws, and on applying information to other problems.

Lower Quality of Teaching Materials. The third major trend influencing classroom interactions is the weakening content of textbooks. There is more material to cover in the same constraints of space and time. Thus new texts cover less and less about more and more. They are condensed to bare facts and summaries and merely annotate major events and important ideas. Why and how these things occurred is neglected.

Typically, textbooks give no indication of the effort that went into major discoveries, ideas, inventions, or decisions. They create the impression that these things happened because of luck or serendipity.

Authors must make selections from all there is to learn about a subject. Thus places, inventions, events, ideas, and people discussed in these textbooks are included as being representative of larger ideas or issues. Teachers have a responsibility to use questions that enable students to recognize that a particular example is representative of something greater and that the process used in studying that example can be transferred to the study of any similar topic.

Teachers must formulate questions that give students insight into the way discoveries, inventions, and decisions are developed. Students should gain an appreciation for the perseverance and relentless curiosity that innovation and discovery require, and they should develop the work habits that are fundamental to creative pursuits. Students also need to recognize the limitations of textbooks and understand the rationale behind an author's choices.

Preparing Students for Work and Continued Education. Questioning skills are central to helping students develop such thinking skills as creative thinking, decision making, problem solving, mental visualization, knowing how to learn, and reasoning. They also can help students acquire responsibility, self-esteem, sociability, self-management, honesty, and integrity. In a 1992 report, the Secretary of Labor's Commission on Achieving Necessary Skills (SCANS) listed these skills along with reading, writing, arithmetic, listening, and speaking as necessary for those entering the workplace.

Questions in Real Life

Think of how people use questions in their daily lives. Examine the reasons for asking questions.

People ask questions usually because they simply do not know the answer. They may need the answer to make a decision. They may want to compare another person's answer to their own beliefs, knowledge, or values.

Questions in real life have practical reasons. The questioner may need to know a simple fact. Or the questioner may desire to know what someone else knows, thinks, feels, or believes. The questioner may need to learn something new or to understand other points of view.

However, most questions asked in the classroom are not based on the real needs or interests of either the teacher or the students. The teacher likely knows the answers to the questions, thus the teacher usually does not learn anything new from the response. Because the questions require only single, low-level answers that come from the resources used, the students also do not learn anything new.

On the other hand, almost all questions raised by students, both in and out of the classroom, have a practical purpose. They are used to get permission, to make plans, to relieve anxiety, to satisfy an interest, to get directions, or to learn something new. Students' real-life questions can be used to get to know someone, to learn about others' experiences, to resolve a controversy, or to make a decision.

There are six essential reasons for asking questions:

1. Curiosity or interest. What questions are asked by inventors or explorers that lead to action? Think about Columbus or Edison.
2. Need for explanation. What questions does a person ask who wants to learn how to make or fix something? Think about Henry Ford.
3. Basis for a decision. What questions must a person ask before making a decision or taking action, particularly when it affects others? Think about Harry Truman.
4. Dissatisfaction with a condition. What questions will lead to improvement of a situation or condition? Think about Clara Barton.
5. Discrepancy between new information and what is known or believed. What questions probe or challenge long-held beliefs? Think about Curie or Pasteur.
6. Need or desire to develop a new skill. What questions will assist in the acquisition of new understandings? Think about the Wright brothers.

Students experience these conditions daily. Questions to meet these conditions are routine among friends, relatives, merchants, bosses, employees, professionals, and colleagues. The teacher's task is to transfer these real-life conditions for questioning to the classroom.

Why Ask Better Questions?

A question calls for interaction. It is an invitation for another to contribute to a discussion, decision, or solution. Asking someone a question assumes that person has information or expertise about a topic. It demonstrates respect for and confidence in others' knowledge, ideas, and opinions. And asking a question often is the key to raising more questions.

Questions are one of the major instructional strategies teachers use throughout the year. Bryce B. Hudgins (1977) estimates that teachers ask 50 questions per period, or 350 per day. However, that frequency in questions indicates that the questions are fact-based and allow little opportunity for higher-level thinking or application.

Teachers have a responsibility to pose questions that elicit high-quality responses from students and that cause students to ask more questions. Students must not be taught that the only important information is what teachers ask about. The content of a teacher's questions will determine what students perceive as important. Low-level questions call for only factual information; and if these are the only questions that are asked, students will believe that correct, right, single answers are most important. However, questions that prompt students to use their knowledge, experiences, backgrounds, beliefs, and intuition will give students a broader perspective and a sense of importance from contributing original ideas.

Effective questions are not just asked. They have to be designed. Much thought needs to be invested in planning questions to meet specific outcomes. Teachers need to analyze the aims of the questions, plan how the questions will be posed, and anticipate how to handle both expected and unexpected responses.

Because questions are fundamental to education, improving questioning skills is fundamental to any restructuring of education. Other restructuring efforts will be a waste of time if they result only in more low-level questions.

Teachers can improve their questioning to initiate higher-level thinking among students. To do so, teachers must become models for students to improve their own questioning abilities. Teachers must design questions that motivate students to gather facts, data, and information. They must help students interpolate, interpret, and extrapolate in order to understand the full implications of what is presented. Teachers must inspire students to see the big picture — the concepts, generalizations, laws, and principles — so they can apply these lessons to future learning.

Questions must be designed to ensure that students understand the full context of important information and its significance. Questions also should give students the opportunity to contribute to their own learning. But to avoid condemning students to information overload, teachers must re-examine what is essential and what is not.

The intent of education is to foster students' desire and ability to be lifelong learners. Thus questioning strategies must provide students with the processes and skills to adapt to changes throughout their lives, and students should be given frequent practice in these processes and skills. When teachers master the art of questioning, they will do more than just equip their students with general knowledge and skills. They will add purpose and relevance to learning.

CHAPTER TWO

Questions as Motivators

Teachers are concerned with increasing student participation, and so the questions they use must be interesting enough that students want to respond. Questions that ask for higher-level thinking will increase student participation.

When planning lessons, teachers should evaluate the questions they intend to ask. Good questions require reflection before they can be answered. While they should be drawn from material that has been learned in class or homework, they also should promote further inquiry; that is, they should be challenging and should inspire more questions. In order to be sure that the questions will grab students' attention, the questions should be open-ended, with more than one viable answer. Such questions will stimulate thought and lead to discussion or debate, which in turn will lead students into learning new information.

Questions also should take into consideration the students' levels of knowledge and allow for their personal input. In addition, questions should determine what students do and do not know. In order to accomplish this, teachers must provide enough time for students to think and respond, and the questions must be designed with these outcomes in mind.

Six Motivation Strategies

The approach that teachers use can affect how much students participate in asking and answering questions. Listed below are strategies that can motivate students to participate.

Ask Fewer Questions. There is an inverse relationship between the number of questions that are asked and the level of thinking required to answer those questions. Research indicates that most teachers ask 50 to 70 questions during a single class session. That many questions require quick, factual, and low-level answers. The purpose of this type of question usually is to verify that students have memorized information. Asking fewer questions, but ones that call for thinking or application, will promote student participation and interaction.

When the teacher asks most of the questions, students perceive that they learn the information only to satisfy the teacher. This reduces their feelings of responsibility for and their involvement in their own learning. Instead, students also should be encouraged to ask questions. Not only does this encourage the students to participate, but the insight that students exhibit in their questions often will be a valuable resource for the teacher.

Teachers should plan carefully the questions they will ask. Four or five good, open-ended questions should be sufficient for each class period, as multiple students will have opportunities to offer answers and discussion. These questions should call on students to apply, react to, or reflect on the content. If these questions do not evoke the desired level of response from the students, then teachers can fall back on questions that elicit the information needed to answer the higher-level questions.

Provide Time for Answers. The differences in the thinking abilities shown by students often is determined by the time they are given to think about their responses. The ability to formulate a response to a question is as much a function of time as it is of intelligence. Unfortunately, research indicates that teachers wait an average of only one second for a student to answer a question before they call on another student (Rowe 1974). Mary Budd Rowe also found that a three- to four-second lapse following a question results in more comprehensive, higher-quality answers. (Of course, this assumes that a higher-level question is asked.) When teachers provide time for their students to think about an answer, more students are able to respond. In addition, providing time for students to think about their answers also conveys to students that thought is important.

Not only should teachers provide time before a student answers a question, they also should provide time after a student responds. If a student's response is brief and simple, allow the student time to elaborate, reason, justify, and support the response. Teachers can use this time to devise a way to cause the interaction to continue.

However, teachers should be aware that students may not interpret the teacher's silence following an answer as a cue for a more complete answer. Often, students have learned that a teacher's silence is an indication that their answer was wrong or unacceptable. The teacher who plans to provide time after a response should let the students know beforehand that this is a strategy to allow students to think more deeply about their answers.

A corollary to allowing more time for a student to answer is allowing time for more students to answer. Thus a teacher should not settle for the first good response to a question. The highly verbal students in a class often are able to provide good answers quickly. If these answers are allowed to close the discussion, deeper and varied thinking might be suppressed. Stating, "These initial ideas are good, but let's see what other possibilities there are," develops the idea that it is worthwhile to delay decisions in order to explore many avenues. It also recognizes that other students need time to explore their thoughts. Also, the final choice of an answer often will be drawn from the various suggestions made by students, thus instilling a sense of collaboration.

Pay Attention to the Student. A student who is answering a question should be the focus of attention in the room. You can demonstrate this by maintaining eye contact with that student and directing the attention of the rest of the class to that student.

Another problem occurs when a teacher habitually repeats questions or students' responses. When this is a pattern, students

learn to pay less attention, because they know the question or response will be repeated. Not only is this a waste of time; it also
can cause the students who do answer to wonder why they were
asked in the first place.

Teachers must develop an atmosphere in which students are
expected to pay attention to their classmates. This is easier to
achieve with open-ended questions, especially those that require
personal experiences, reactions, or opinions. By routinely asking
students to comment on, critique, or analyze another student's
response, teachers provide a valid reason for the class to pay
attention to the responses.

To ensure that the class pays attention to the student who is
answering a question, teachers should ask students to speak so
others can hear. The teacher also may stand at a distance from the
student answering the question. When a teacher stands too close
to responders, they often lower their voice and direct their
answers solely to the teacher.

To facilitate eye contact and interaction, one method is to seat
students so that half of the class is facing the other half. In this
way, the teacher no longer is the focal point. When teachers maintain a relative distance between themselves and the student answering a question, and when they maintain eye contact with the
student, they can transform a one-on-one conversation into a
class discussion.

Talk Less. When a teacher is lecturing, students are passive. A
teacher who dominates the class time gives the impression that
students are just vessels waiting to be filled. Consequently, students come to believe that their role is only to listen, rather than
to become active participants in learning.

Lecturing does have some positive and productive uses. The
following criteria can help teachers determine when a lecture is
appropriate:

- The information is not intended for long-term retention or
  memorization.
- The information is unavailable in any other instructional form.
- The information is to be used as a bridge to further material.

- The objective is to motivate or arouse students' interest or to provoke responses.
- The information demonstrates divergent viewpoints for follow-up discussion.

Another common problem among teachers is to answer their own questions when students respond too slowly. Teachers often submit to this bad habit in order to complete a lesson on time, but it conveys to students that their participation is not a priority in the class. Instead, teachers should break the question into smaller questions or rephrase it when students do not respond.

There are several strategies that teachers can use to refrain from answering their own questions.

1. Have on hand alternate or lead-in questions that will help students answer the original question.
2. Approach the question from a different viewpoint.
3. Encourage students to say so when they are confused by a question or when they just do not know the answer.

Give Students Time to Write Answers. Another motivational strategy is to provide time for students to begin to write answers to their questions before responding aloud. This writing time offers a reflective pause, and it gives students time to prepare an answer. This strategy helps students who process ideas more slowly or deliberately and are not able to respond quickly "on the spot." Another advantage is that, if a student says, "That's what I was going to say," there is proof.

Activate Background Knowledge. Before changing topics or introducing new ideas, give students the background knowledge they will need to connect the new material with what they already know. This strategy lays the groundwork for better questions and answers because students are not taken by surprise by the new information.

Overcoming Student Reluctance

As students get older, they often become reluctant to answer questions in class. This is especially likely when the questions call for precise answers.

Students employ several strategies to avoid classroom participation, but the ultimate strategy is to become an "I don't know" student. Older students may see "not knowing" an answer to be safer than risking an incorrect or unacceptable answer that exposes them to ridicule by either the teacher or the class. These students probably have used two other strategies before reaching this phase: avoiding eye contact with the teacher as the question is posed and, if that is ineffective, looking busy as the teacher decides on whom to call.

It is a teacher's responsibility to engage the "I don't know" student. The following interaction illustrates a strategy that has worked for many teachers, particularly in secondary grades. The teacher has asked Bill to stay after class to discuss his lack of participation in classroom discussions.

Teacher: Bill, I see that you have fallen into the habit of saying, "I don't know," when you're asked a question. I want to help you break that habit. You heard what the assignment is; here's the question I'm going to ask you in class tomorrow. [Pauses] And here is the answer.

By focusing on "habit," the emphasis is not on Bill as a bad person or a poor student. In addition, Bill now knows that the teacher knows that he does know the answer.

The next day the teacher calls on Bill to answer the question they reviewed. The teacher is firm in getting him to answer. This scene is repeated until the teacher senses that Bill is feeling comfortable answering and that other students recognize his contributions.

Several days later, the teacher and Bill again speak privately after class.

Teacher: Bill, you know what the assignment is. Here is the question I'm going to ask in class tomorrow. [Pauses] Bill, do you want the answer?

When Bill refuses the answer, it is because he now feels secure in his own ability to attempt to answer. During the next few weeks, the teacher observes Bill becoming increasingly comfortable about participating. The teacher again asks to see Bill after class.

Teacher: Bill, you know what the assignment is. Do you want to see the question I'm going to ask in class tomorrow?

When Bill says no, the habit has been broken. Trust and safety have been established between Bill and his teacher. A new habit — participating — has been substituted for "I don't know."

Teachers are able to identify the reasons for students' reluctance to be involved in class. That is the first step to overcoming the problem. The second step is to identify strategies to motivate students to participate. Different strategies need to be used for different students. Following are some common reasons students have for not participating in class and strategies teachers can use to overcome the problem.

- The student is afraid to fail. Let students know that not knowing something simply indicates an area where something can be learned.
- The student is afraid of ridicule. Do not allow students to put down other's answers.
- The student lacks confidence because of past failures. Help students succeed by asking questions you think they can answer, by rephrasing, by including information in the question, or by asking students to respond from their own experiences.
- The student is unsure of the expected response. Provide study guides or a list of questions for the week.
- The student is afraid to speak in class. Allow time for students to discuss the material in a small group before you address questions to the entire class.
- The student is uninterested in the topic or is apathetic. Make connections between the material and students' lives. Ask provocative or evocative questions. Ask for students' feelings, beliefs, and experiences, rather than just facts.
- The student is unwilling to be labeled a "brain" by other students. Create a classroom atmosphere in which knowledge is shared, not exhibited. Ask questions that call for personal reactions instead of facts.

- The question is too complex or is unclear. Rephrase the question or encourage students to ask clarifying questions. An alternative strategy is to provide questions ahead of time.
- The question is above the student's level of experience or is intimidating to the student. Break the question into parts. Ask one question at a time, with one focus.
- The answer is expected too quickly. Allow three to four seconds for a student to answer.
- The student does not know the answer. Rephrase and simplify the question. Accept simple answers that contribute to the broader answer.
- The student finds the answer difficult to express. Help students interpret their answers by restating them. Ask other students how they interpret the response.

In addition to being reluctant to answer teachers' questions, many students also are reluctant to ask questions of the teacher. The reasons for their reluctance to ask questions often are similar to their reasons for not answering teachers' questions.

To encourage students to ask questions, teachers should establish an open, humane, and supportive classroom atmosphere. Teachers should prohibit students from putting down those who ask questions. And they should emphasizes that questions not only are acceptable, but they are expected. Student questions demonstrate that learning is taking place.

Teachers should provide frequent opportunities for students' questions throughout the period. They should compliment students for asking good questions and encourage them to ask more questions. To ensure that students ask good questions, teachers should model the level of questions they expect from students.

One strategy that teachers can use to encourage students to ask questions is to ask students to write their questions one or two weeks before the beginning of a new unit. Collect their questions or call on students to read them. The questions can be written individually or by small groups of students. Post a list of the questions, and ask students to respond to each other's ideas.

Using such strategies to overcome obstacles to student participation should be a priority for teachers. Often, students will show several of the problems listed above. Begin with the most obvious problems.

Finding Time for Better Questions

Many teachers believe that taking time to ask higher-level questions can be done only at the expense of covering the text material. However, teachers should remember that they are not obligated to cover a text entirely. Nor will any text include all or most of the material needed to meet a district's curriculum objectives. Instead, teachers need to decide what information should be eliminated or substituted in order to provide time for higher-level thinking and real applications of the content.

The district committee that chooses texts can lend support in making these decisions. The committee should determine guidelines for effectively using the texts. These guidelines might include:

1. Identifying the "big ideas" that the text can promote in that discipline.
2. Noting the topics or ideas that may have been included in previous grades or texts, in order to reduce duplication.
3. Identifying topics or ideas that have not been introduced or included in previous texts or grades.
4. Identifying the match between the objectives of the district curriculum guides and the text.
5. Specifying similarities among what is emphasized in the texts, curriculum guides, and standardized tests.

This information will provide the direction teachers need for what material to cover, thus providing them with more time to develop questioning strategies. Unfortunately, some district committees do not provide these guidelines. In that case the responsibility for these decisions rests with the teacher.

The district teachers who develop the curriculum guides determine the content to be covered. This is the level at which it should be decided whether to promote low-level objectives or more comprehensive ideas and applications. It is incumbent on these district curriculum leaders to set standards that emphasize the identification and understanding of concepts, generalizations, laws, and principles, rather than only facts. They should incorporate the outcomes of higher-level thinking skills and the application of text material, thus giving classroom teachers more direction for designing questions to fulfill those outcomes.

One common concern among teachers is that by covering less material more deeply, they are putting their students at a disadvantage when taking standardized tests. In addition, the students' lower scores on these tests may be considered a reflection of the teacher's skills.

However, no test adequately measures the content of any textbook. For example, one study found very little correlation between the content of standardized tests in mathematics and the content of the leading mathematics textbooks. It is true that standardized test scores may reflect on the teacher, but the odds of students doing better simply as a result of a teacher "covering" a given text or curriculum guide are small. In addition, as developers design tests that measure more than just facts, this may become even less of a concern.

Teachers also should remember that there is more to students' test-taking skills than just knowledge of content. Students' "test wisdom" also contributes to their success on tests. The way students are questioned in the classroom will have an effect on the scores they achieve on tests. For example, the spelling section of standardized tests usually asks students to select the correctly spelled word from a list and to fill in their choice on the test form. However, spelling tests in the classroom usually are administered verbally by the teacher. If the students have not experienced the method used in standardized tests, they can be penalized more by their unfamiliarity with the method than by their lack of knowledge.

Four Conditions for Effective Questioning

Questions must meet four conditions in order to promote participation and higher-level thinking.

An Issue, Problem, or Challenge. First, there must be something to think about. Factual information from texts must be looked at in terms of problems to solve, issues to be resolved, decisions to be made, and interests and needs to be satisfied. Questions also might pose dilemmas, uncertainties, and paradoxes about the topic for further analysis.

Corresponding Reference Points. Second, there must be points of reference that coincide with the problem, such as facts, data, and observations. Students have a variety of experiences that may have some relationships to a topic. They have reactions, opinions, feelings, attitudes, values, and beliefs. Biases and emotions also should be examined. It is important to use their ideas about their world as a reference point. In order for students to analyze and understand the biases or prejudices that affect their learning, teachers must use skillfully planned questioning strategies to increase their powers of observation and reduce or overcome misconceptions and errors.

An Appropriate Approach. Third, questioning must promote different ways of thinking. The term ways of thinking is used, rather than the usual thinking skills, to emphasize the difference between engaging in a type of thinking, such as comparing, summarizing, or interpreting, and the skill required or demonstrated in using it. Students may choose different approaches, depending on whether the goal is to learn a new skill, to solve a problem, or to test a hypothesis.

A Reasoning Goal. The fourth, and perhaps most important, condition for effective questioning is that there is a reason to think about the material. It is a mistake to think the product of learning is merely an accumulation of knowledge. That would be like loading a cargo ship in New York and then letting it sit there. The cargo would become useless. The same is true of knowledge that stops with facts.

CHAPTER THREE

Designing Questions

Asking questions and designing questions are not the same thing. Designing questions implies that there are clear, definite objectives and that the sequence or pattern of questioning will increase both teachers' and students' chances of achieving those ends. The word "design" also implies that the questions should avoid appearing random or aimless. Thus teachers first must select the objectives to be achieved through questioning, then they can design the sequence of questions that will lead students to those objectives.

Anatomy of a Question

Before designing questions, it is helpful to understand clearly the "anatomy" of a question — that is, what gives rise to a question, how the question is framed, and what answer or response is intended or anticipated.

Eight considerations are helpful:

1. What is the origin, purpose, or reason for the question?
2. From what source(s) does the question arise?
3. How does the questioner determine which questions to ask and in what order?
4. What criteria should the question meet?
5. How might students think about the question or approach answering it?

6. What kinds of responses might students make?
7. How will the teacher treat students' responses?
8. What follow-up questions might the student or teacher ask on the basis of the initial question?

These considerations are useful when examining individual questions or sequences of questions and anticipated responses. After all, in almost every case, more must be done than just designing individual questions. Teachers also must design a questioning *strategy*. A strategy is a carefully planned set of questions that uses a sequence of steps to lead to the achievement of the instructional objectives. Teachers can ensure that a sound strategy is planned by:

1. Writing questions while planning the unit of work,
2. Analyzing what a question asks the student to do in regard to knowledge and skills,
3. Trying out the strategy to determine the degree to which it is successful in generating student participation, and
4. Ascertaining the quality of students' responses, then modifying the questioning strategies as needed.

In designing questions, the teacher must decide when to emphasize content objectives, when to emphasize process objectives, and when to emphasize both. This usually is determined by the circumstances. The balance between content and process must be dynamic, changing to meet the objectives of the class. At times, content may be more important, such as in preparing a foundation for new learning. For example, in learning about health and safety, content takes precedence because the information is so essential. In other situations, process — that is, learning how to learn — will be more important. However, though either process or content may take precedence in a given situation, neither should be ignored in the overall questioning strategy.

Another set of objectives that affects the questioning strategy involves determining which learning will be required for only a short term and which will be for long-term purposes. Some learning is topic-specific; other learning is necessary for understanding related topics. For example, the study of natural resources in a particular geographic area is valuable only when discussing that area. However, the study of conditions that produce those natural resources or products will be applicable to the study of other areas as well. The fact that Colombia is a major producer of coffee (specific, short-term knowledge) is not as important as having the students identify the conditions that enable coffee to be grown there (general, long-term knowledge).

Questioning strategies that differentiate between objectives ultimately affect the types of evaluations that the teacher will conduct. In addition, these questioning strategies will enable students to see that learning is more than just memorization and will increase their interest in the information.

Teachers also should take into account the characteristics of the particular group of students when designing questions. Different groups of students will require different strategies.

There are a variety of purposes for asking questions. Questions can be used to motivate students to learn a new topic, to analyze information they are learning, to evaluate what they have learned, and to serve many other purposes.

Different researchers advocate different strategies for questioning. Some suggest asking questions at the beginning of a lesson. Others suggest stopping the students during a lesson to ask questions. And others suggest waiting until the end of class to ask questions. However, the purpose of a questioning strategy will determine the timing of the questions. Thus it is more appropriate to ask some types of questions before a new unit of study, some types during the unit, and some after.

Teachers should keep in mind that the attitude in which questions are asked also helps to determine how — or, indeed, whether — students respond. Facial expression and tone of voice convey attitudes. If students perceive questioning as "interrogation," "grilling," or "cross-examining," they are likely to be less responsive or to respond negatively. On the other hand, if students are asked to "explore," "contemplate," or "analyze," they are more likely to view the questioning as open and inviting, and they will respond positively.

Questioning Before Study Begins

Certain questioning strategies should be used before starting a new unit of study. Some of the more important purposes for these questions are:

To Motivate. Several criteria must be considered in order to motivate students. First, students must feel that they have some control over their learning. Thus teachers need to design their questions accordingly.

Teachers must make the material interesting by introducing something that will challenge the students. They also should keep these introductions interesting by using a variety of approaches throughout the year. For example, they can begin units with surveys, panel discussions, debates, role playing, or simulations. They might begin with an audiovisual presentation, speakers or visitors, or field trips. Or they might pose situations that are perplexing, that present conflicting accounts, that contradict typical biases or stereotypes, or that require students to solve a mystery. In studying material with unknown outcomes, students can be asked to make predictions, identify trends, or use their creativity or imagination to anticipate the outcomes. Other topics will allow the use of questions that require students to reflect on how their own experiences relate to the topic.

To Promote Student Goal Setting. Teachers not only must be concerned with their desired goals for instruction but also must use questioning to engage students in setting their own goals. This provides students with additional ways to have autonomy in their own learning. It also allows all students to see the range and levels of their classmates' goals, which may serve as a guide for setting their own goals. In addition, it conveys to the students that it is acceptable to indicate a desire to learn.

To Determine Readiness. Once the teacher has set the objectives and has determined the knowledge and skills students need to begin the unit, the teacher will need to use pretesting strategies to determine the skills and knowledge students can bring to the subject.

Students are at a disadvantage if they have no experience with or little knowledge about the material that is about to be introduced. One strategy to familiarize students is to present them with a problem (Should the United States military get involved in other countries' disputes?) or an issue (Should Little Red Riding Hood have been sent to her grandmother's house alone?). This can be done by posing scenarios or with simulations drawn from what will be studied. Alternatively, teachers might make provocative statements or present situations that call for reactions; or they can provide students with commitment-statement worksheets, which require students to declare a position on the topic. Student responses can then be used as a study guide for the new material.

Preparatory questions also can require students to use their imaginations to anticipate the new unit. The teacher can provide a brief description or visual aids from the unit to get them started.

To Stimulate Thinking. At times, teachers might need to provide students with practice in particular ways of thinking before they begin a new unit. To accomplish this, questions must be worded carefully so that students will learn that a particular type of thinking is expected. The teacher also must ask questions to determine that students understand the characteristics and skills that a particular type of thinking requires. These questions should be designed not only to identify students' skills in that way of thinking but also to increase their level of expertise.

One important thinking skill that students will need is identifying patterns in the content. This enables students to make predictions about the material and to anticipate how the study will evolve. Pattern recognition also allows them to see relationships to prior material and to focus on the new content in a structured manner, which also will enhance their study. In mathematics, for example, questions should focus on identifying problems so that students learn to determine the method, algorithm, or process to be used. When studying literature, questions that alert students to propaganda techniques and patterns will help them discriminate between objective and slanted material and help them to recognize an author's intent.

To Convey Purpose. Students should be made aware of objectives and anticipated outcomes and how these will aid further learning, relate to their lives, enable them to use the learning, or prepare them to do something new or better as a result. Using questions to demonstrate the continuing value of learning will increase their attention and motivate them to retain the information. These questions also can demonstrate that what students previously learned still has value and that the students are not "done with learning about" the previous lessons.

To Create a Positive Learning Atmosphere. There is an obvious difference between having to learn and wanting to learn. It is important that students know there is safety and comfort in the classroom and that they will be treated humanely when they do contribute. The pace of learning has to seem unhurried, accompanied by a willingness on the part of the teacher to provide help and elaboration where needed. The students must feel that the teacher is interested in them as individuals as well as students. Students also must feel that their views, positions, or biases may be expressed and discussed, rather than judged according to another's criteria. The questioning strategy that a teacher uses can help to develop that atmosphere.

To Discern Student Interest or Knowledge. How do we know what students have learned or want to learn unless we consider what they already know or are interested in? Teachers need to give students opportunities to ask questions before they begin to study in earnest.

To Activate Background Knowledge. Having discerned what students know, we can build on that foundation and more fully use the texts, curriculum guides, and so forth that are designed to add to students' knowledge and understandings. The questions in this case are focused on the "fit" of new knowledge with existing understandings.

The "Big Four" Questions

Perhaps one of the most important reasons to ask questions before a new unit of study is to activate students' existing knowledge that relates to the material. To do this, teachers should ask the

"Big Four" questions. These questions establish where to start instruction and how far it can be taken. The Big Four questions are:

1. What do you already know about the new topic?
2. What do you think you know?
3. What do you want to know?
4. What do you feel or believe about an issue or problem?

Responses to the first two questions — What do you know? and What do you think you know? — identify students' knowledge or misconceptions, so that adjustments can be made in the questioning strategy. By asking, "What do you think you know?" the teacher shows students that it is permissible to guess and, even more important, to risk being wrong. That creates an openness in which important information about their knowledge is revealed.

If the material is unfamiliar to students, by asking, "What do you want to know?" the teacher gives students some autonomy and input into their learning and incentives for putting forth the effort to learn. Involving the students in questioning from the beginning fosters the sense that they are a community of learners, not learning the material just to satisfy the teacher. When they hear their classmates' questions, students also learn about the range of interests within the group.

This question serves several other purposes. First, it enables a teacher to assess the levels of students' questions. If most of the students' responses are low-level, fact-based questions, the teacher will need to train the students in forming higher-level questions. On the other hand, when they ask higher-level questions, the teacher should acknowledge them in order to reinforce such questions.

Students often will ask for information that goes beyond that provided in the basic text. This provides the opportunity for students to learn that no single text has all the information about a topic. It creates the need to seek additional sources if students want complete answers to their questions.

Determining what students want to know about a topic also has another important purpose. With this question, teachers can determine not only students' interests, but also their level of interest in the new information. This serves two important objectives. First, students learn that the teacher is aware that their interests vary and that the teacher is secure enough to allow them to say so. Second, determining the students' levels of interest enables the teacher to devise alternative plans to capitalize on the levels of individual and group interest.

When an issue or problem is the focus of learning, asking the question, "What do you feel or believe about this issue or problem?" allows the teacher to consider students' opinions when planning the questioning strategy. These opinions usually fall in at least two categories: those related to students' personal lives and those related to societal issues that students will someday face.

It is not the teacher's role to assume responsibility for changing students' personal opinions. Rather, the teacher's responsibility is to use questioning strategies that will provide students with processes with which to understand the bases for their beliefs, feelings, and opinions. These processes should emphasize the steps of analysis, evaluation, or reflection, which students can use throughout their lives. However, teachers must tread very carefully when student opinions are based on religion or family values.

The fourth question also can be phrased more broadly in order to diffuse a student's fear of expressing a personal opinion. Thus the teacher might ask, "What do you think other people believe about this issue or problem?" This allows a student to express an opinion without being forced to defend it or to continue to advocate it long after the student has changed his or her mind. In addition, this form of the question also enables other students to agree, refute, elaborate, or give another viewpoint without reflecting personally on each other. It is likely that the responses to this form of the question will be the same as if the teacher asked about the students' personal beliefs. However, these responses will not be viewed as personal.

These "Big Four" questions also have an important purpose for students. If the students' responses and questions are recorded — for example, on a large chart — and posted in the room, they become a study guide. Students can determine whether their own responses were accurate, whether their questions were answered, and whether the opinions stated at the beginning of the unit were supported or need to be explored further.

It is important to remember that there are three objectives that should be met by teachers' questions before a new unit begins. The first objective is to elicit knowledge that is specific to the particular topic and applicable to subsequent learning. The second purpose of these questions is to teach students a strategy for learning about any topic. The third objective is to cause students to understand the consequences of learning, that is, how to apply knowledge and develop thinking skills.

The Timing of Preparatory Questions

The timing of preparatory questions is important. Unfortunately, a common approach is to complete a unit of work with a test on Friday or the day before a holiday, then begin a new unit on Monday or when classes resume. This practice leaves no time for preparatory questions.

A better approach is to begin preparatory questions two or three days before a unit is introduced in the primary grades and two to three weeks in advance in grades four and up. In the meantime, students can use such resources as the school library to learn something about the topic.

Students can use the Big Four questions to structure their investigations before the unit begins. For example, most students will find that they do know something about the topic; and if students work collectively, soon they all will know what each student knew, thereby enlarging their knowledge base without formal instruction. Their responses to the question, "What do you want to know?" can provide their personal study guides. Also, their expressed feelings or opinions can be compared with their beliefs after they have examined the problem or issue. Because the students will share their responses to the Big Four questions with other students, they each will gain additional perspectives, questions, and interests.

The major benefit to students when they consistently use the Big Four questions over several grade levels is that they may consciously begin to use them whenever they study something new, both in school and throughout their lives.

The Big Four questions benefit teachers in several ways. All teachers prepare a general lesson plan for the unit to be studied. When teachers use the Big Four questions far enough in advance of a unit, they can use the student responses to personalize their plan for that class. If a student has advanced knowledge about the upcoming unit, the teacher can find out in time to make special plans for that student, either by using that student to help the rest of the class or by planning a special assignment for that student. In addition, the teacher can use the students' responses to the Big Four questions not only to take their interests into account when planning the lesson but also to gather additional resources that complement those interests.

Questioning During Lessons

Interjecting questions during a lesson can be appropriate when the entire class is listening to a lecture, viewing an audiovisual presentation, watching a demonstration, or participating in an experiment. When students are working individually or in small groups, it is not a good time to interrupt them with questions because of their different learning paces. Written questions are effective for activities that involve individual reading or writing, since they allow for such variations. Different strategies should be tried in a variety of situations to determine the most productive approaches for your classroom.

The purpose of questioning during a lesson differs from other categories of questions, whether the lessons involve reading, viewing, practice, or listening. In this case, the teacher's purposes should be:

- To inspire *thinking and reflection* as learning takes place,
- To allow students to *review material* as learning progresses,
- To involve students in *evaluating* their understanding of implicit and explicit learning,

- To encourage them to *"think ahead"* — to predict, anticipate, and identify trends or patterns.

The following question types and strategies can be used to accomplish the above purposes.

Analyzing and Critiquing. Students must learn that anything that calls for reading, viewing, practice, or listening also calls for analyzing and critiquing. Analyzing requires students to think about the parts of the learning and how they fit together. Critiquing uses criteria to evaluate material in such areas as completeness, organization, logic, believability, applicability, validity, consistency, and relevance. Through providing practice opportunities for developing these skills and designing questions with which students may use them, the teacher demonstrates that learning is an active process.

The questioning strategies must lead students to become skeptics about information. When students are taught to just accept the information they are given, they can become cynics when they learn the way the world is, rather than the way it often is presented in school. As an example, the way that a bill becomes a law is outlined very objectively in texts, but little is said about the political machinations that determine how a bill really becomes a law. When students learn that the world often works differently, such as during the 2000 presidential election, they may respond with cynicism and distrust. Using strategies in which students may raise their own questions about new material, ideas, events, and situations will motivate them to seek answers, as opposed to letting their acceptance of information lead to cynicism.

Students can be given practice in analyzing and critiquing through an assignment that requires them to react to something they read. For each section of the assignment, they choose from several possible reactions and place a symbol for that reaction beside the selection. Students evaluate each section of the assignment according to the following statements:

- I doubt this, or I have questions to ask about this.
- I would like to know more about this.

- I don't believe this.
- There are more considerations and conditions that apply.
- I don't understand this part.
- I detect bias or prejudice here.
- This is important.
- This needs more support to be believed or understood.
- I can think of other applications or uses.
- I can't relate this to my life or to the world today.

Each of the above statements would have a symbol, such as a star, a cross, or question mark, that the student would mark on the reading selection. The use of symbols causes students to focus on the assignment. Also, the students' explanations of why they used the symbols can help the teacher in planning further questioning strategies.

These statements and their symbols also can be adapted to assignments other than reading. For example, if the students are viewing a videotape or film, they can take notes and add the symbols to their notes. The number of symbols and their level of sophistication can be adapted to fit the grade level.

Anticipating Outcomes. Another basis for questioning during learning is to prompt students to make predictions and anticipate outcomes. This enables them to compare what they anticipated with what actually occurs, and thus to examine how well they paid attention to the background material. It also allows them to analyze progress in their ability to anticipate or predict. This technique can lead to the use of higher-level thinking skills as students compare the validity and quality of their predictions with the real outcomes.

When students are asked to practice making decisions, choosing solutions to problems, or resolving issues, they must learn to examine the consequences of the alternatives they postulate. Examining consequences is a valuable process with which to evaluate their ideas.

In addition, skillful questions can help students to identify trends and to draw conclusions from a lesson. The teacher's questions should alert students to important details in the lesson so they will be able to draw conclusions about an expected outcome.

Summarizing. The teacher should ask questions that encourage students to summarize segments of material, particularly after each chapter or unit. In this way, the students will become aware of how the information is organized.

Questioning also can encourage students to relate the material to what they have previously learned, as well as to their lives or to society.

Detecting Bias and Examining Viewpoints. When resources are used that may be biased, students should be encouraged to respond with their beliefs or feelings. The teacher's questions should guide them to perceive indications of bias in texts, lectures, visual aids, and even their own discussions.

Teachers also need to encourage students to examine new or different points of view. One effective way to do that is to use situations from real life for which students gather information from the many points of view involved in making a decision. Teachers also can present a historical decision in the form of a dilemma and then ask students to take the roles of different groups or individuals involved in making the decision. This is also a good approach to assess and reinforce learning at the end of a lesson or unit.

Questions After the Lesson

Questions asked after the lesson immediately reinforce the learning. They help the teacher ascertain that students have identified the major ideas and provide additional practice for students in the skills taught in the lesson. They will allow students to apply or use the material. And these questions can develop students' thinking skills by prompting them to summarize, draw conclusions, and critique the accuracy and completeness of the content.

Questions asked after the lesson also can help students understand their own thought processes. This process calls for students to answer such questions as:

- Were my goals for learning reached?

- Did I learn what was to be learned?
- To what degree were my methods of learning productive? To what degree were my work habits productive?
- What would I change to improve my learning?
- Was my opinion changed?
- What ideas will have to be considered further?
- What do I know now, or what can I do now, because of the learning?

Teachers can give students the questions at the beginning of the lesson so that they can think about them and discuss them after the lesson is over. Also questions that call for students to reflect on what they have learned can be asked after the lesson.

There are a variety of uses for questions asked after the lesson. Some of those uses and sample questions are:

1. To determine consequences of actions, ideas, and situations.
   - What will happen now?
   - Who is or was affected?
   - What problems could arise?
   - What are the positive and negative consequences?
   - What factors might have changed the outcome?

2. To summarize.
   - What were the main features?
   - What are the most important outcomes?
   - Who had the most effect on the outcome?
   - What needed to be considered?

3. To identify examples or analogies.
   - What else is this like?

4. To reflect on what was learned.
   - What can be applied to other situations?
   - What does this learning have in common with what you have learned before?
   - How does it apply to our lives?

5. To draw conclusions.
   - What is the value of this learning?
   - What have you learned that can be applied to your lives?
   - What skill or mastery have you acquired?

6. To synthesize information and use it, along with past learning, in new ways.
   - What new or different thoughts or ideas did you have?

7. To extend students' learning.
   - What information do you need to satisfy your understanding?
   - What new questions, concerns, or interests arose during the learning?

Asking questions that require student reactions to the entire lesson is also important. For example, students should be required to evaluate the content of the lesson. To do this, they must have questioning strategies that enable them to establish appropriate criteria.

A Combination Strategy

Teachers who involve their students in writing throughout a lesson can use a questioning strategy that combines questions used before, during, and after the lesson. At the beginning of the lesson, the students are asked to respond in writing to an idea. The teacher collects the students' papers and holds them for a few days while the students engage in further study. Then the teacher returns the papers to the students and allows them to make any changes they wish.

In the next class session after the papers are returned, the students are placed in small groups to share their ideas. Then they again are allowed to change their individual written responses. After students have had the chance to write a third draft, the teacher asks such questions as: "Did your reactions change? If yes, in what ways? If no, how were they strengthened?" or "What happened in the intervals that affirmed or changed your reactions? Was there any information that would have caused a change in your initial reactions?" The teacher might provide copies of each draft for comparison.

Evaluating Questions

Designing questions is a skill. As with any skill, criteria are required to determine the level of success in acquiring and using that skill. The following criteria can be used when designing questions:

1. There is differentiation between questions for short-term learning and for long-term learning.
2. The questions enable students to apply what they learned to learning related material.
3. The questions establish relationships with past and future learning.
4. The questions help students to relate the material to their lives or to society by applying it or by making analogies.
5. The questions allow students to see the usefulness of the lesson for applying their new knowledge or being able to do something new.
6. The questions encourage students to use the factual information to develop concepts, generalizations, laws, and principles that can be applied to new learning.
7. The questions provide practice in appropriate and important skills in addition to reinforcing content.
8. The questioning strategy does not ask predominantly for recitation but calls for students to respond individually from the perspective of their own lives.
9. The questions are asked in a way that is nonthreatening and that avoids putting students on the defensive or embarrassing them.
10. The questions convey genuine interest in the way the students respond and in the content of their responses.
11. The questions reveal something about the students or the topic that the teacher did not anticipate or know previously.

Organizing Questions

Once the teacher has established the desired outcomes of a questioning strategy and has designed the specific questions, the teacher needs to decide on the appropriate method of interaction. There are five basic types of interactions, each requiring a different method of organization.

The question-and-answer method of organization is used to ascertain the students' degree of learning of the intended outcomes. In this method, the teacher and students alternate asking and answering questions. Usually, the questions used for this method require single, precise answers that come from the text, lecture, or other type of resource, rather than from the student's own knowledge. This type of session often is referred to as recitation, to distinguish it from discussion.

Open-ended questions ensure more than one response, which allows more students to participate in the answer. One way to accomplish this is to organize students in small groups so that they can share their responses before speaking to the entire class. Otherwise, half of the class should face the other half, which encourages eye contact and interaction among students and takes the focus off the teacher. If the question calls for long, detailed answers, the class can be grouped in pairs that work together on their responses.

Teachers using this type of organization, or any of the types that follow, might wish to ask students to write their responses before they begin work in their groups. This will allow students to be ready to contribute to the group or class discussions. Writing their initial responses, whether only one-word responses or complete essays, encourages the greatest amount of student involvement, because all of the students will be engaged actively in the assignment.

Open-ended questions, whether in the form of problems, issues, or decision-making situations, should meet some of the following criteria.

- They employ previous learning and are applicable to analogous situations.

- They are not constrained by previous learning.
- They call for production or generation, not reiteration, of knowledge.
- They allow for a variety of strategies or approaches by students.
- They allow for a variety of paths to a solution, as well as to a variety of solutions.
- They require justification and support of responses.
- They call for the use of heuristics (problem-solving rules of thumb) versus algorithms (formulas or set processes).
- They do not have a set number of answers or responses.
- They place value on the processes students use to prepare their responses.
- They require students' personal input, based on their experience, judgment, feelings, or study.
- In mathematics, they usually call for multiple steps, or for combining processes in different or new ways.

Discussion sessions can involve students in solving problems, making decisions, or resolving issues. Discussion sessions allow students to contribute based on their knowledge, feelings, beliefs, and experiences. Also, the exchange of ideas and knowledge will inspire reflection by the students.

To promote discussion among students, organize them in small groups of three to five. This provides for a relatively high amount of student involvement. In a class situation, only one of thirty students actively participates at any one time. In groups of five, one out of five students is active at any one time.

Questions from the students can cause them to think about their own learning. To start a session with questions from the students, first ask students to write a given number of questions. This enables them to express their interests, concerns, and positions. After the students have written their questions, it is preferable for them to share their questions with a small group before sharing with the class. A summary report from each small group will save time. These questions, and any that the teacher adds, should be copied for the class. The list then can serve as an outline for the lesson.

Evaluating through questioning can be used by either the teacher or the students. The teacher uses this method to determine how well the students understand a lesson. The teacher also can use this method to evaluate his or her questioning strategy. The students can use this method to examine their own progress. When students have the opportunity to establish the criteria for evaluation, it not only personalizes their evaluations but also provides them with practice in setting criteria for other aspects of their lives.

The goals of learning are the impetus for the types and design of questions that teachers choose. The question strategies determine the method of classroom organization; and the criteria for the design of the questions, and their effectiveness, allow the teacher to monitor students' readiness for the study and to evaluate its effectiveness afterward.

Once these decisions are made, the teacher will be ready to work on strategies for delivering the questions. The next chapter introduces specific questioning strategies.

Ten Sample Lesson Starters

Variations of the Big Four questions can lead to an assortment of ways to begin a lesson. Each of these ways can be an effective way to engage students. Here are some examples:

- Use a commitment list. A commitment list asks students to state their beliefs or feelings about a lesson topic before the lesson begins.
- Ask a provocative question. Evoking a strong student response can motivate the student to study the lesson more closely.
- Set up a debate. Structuring a situation in which students can take pro and con positions can move students to examine facts and arguments carefully.
- Check for understanding. Finding out what students know with simple, initial questions can set the stage for lessons that are easier to understand and better promote student learning.

- Set up a role play. Students become active learners when they have to take on roles heretofore unfamiliar to them.
- Structure student interviews. Students can pair off and interview one another using the Big Four questions.
- Administer a version of the final exam. Using a variation of the final test as a pretest will help students understand the learning goals of the lesson.
- Provide a case study. If the information to be studied is abstract, developing a case study for students to consider can make the information more concrete and relevant to real life.
- Prepare a syllabus or study guide. Putting the "bones" of the lesson on paper is especially helpful, both for students who need a roadmap to the information to be learned and for independent learners who want to work ahead or on related ideas.
- Create a learning activity pack. Sets of learning activities are useful when a topic can be studied in many different ways. They are particularly helpful for individualizing instruction.

CHAPTER FOUR

Specific Questioning Strategies

The following strategies are taken from teacher workshops and commercial programs and have proven effective for a number of years. They engage students in critical and creative thinking, as well as in many other ways of thinking. They provide interaction with others and opportunities to work independently. Very high-level discussions take place during these interactions. Many questions are raised that challenge the students and ask them to support their ideas and explain their reasoning. The questions call for such high-level tactics as persuasion, setting priorities, and using analogies.

The Idea of the Cup

Invention is a frequent theme in classroom instruction. In the "Idea of the Cup" strategy, students are directed to review the history of an invention or innovation, how it might have come about, and how it evolved. This strategy helps students reflect on the positive and negative effects of the invention, to understand that change is a constant, and to learn that both its positive and negative effects must be considered in its evaluation.

This strategy can be used for any invention, performance, or idea. Some of the questions that can be used in this strategy follow.

- Tell how you think the idea of the cup came into being.
- List what you believe was the first cup form, second form, third form, etc.
- What conditions could have created a need for a cup?
- Hypothesize how the creation of the first "formal" cup changed the society into which it was introduced.
- List what you believe may have been some early spin-off creations from the idea of the cup.
- Hypothesize how these spin-off creations may have changed the life of the society at that time.
- Who were the winners and losers when the cup first was introduced? As each advancement in the form of the cup occurred?
- What changes did the cup bring about in society? In the ways that people acted, did things, thought, and believed?
- What needs did the cup meet? What caused the need for the cup to be further developed?
- What needs were reduced or eliminated by the cup?
- What problems or discontent did the cup cause — for whom or what?
- By whom was the cup valued and why?

Three Little Pigs

When students need to examine at least two sides of a problem, such as in a literary dilemma, the "Three Little Pigs" strategy can be used. This strategy requires students to define the problem and to identify the parties to the problem, the victims or beneficiaries, and the roots of the dilemma. It allows them to be flexible and creative in discussing a resolution and to consider changes that would have to occur to achieve a resolution. It also requires students to examine the consequences of these changes. Support or justification of the students' decisions and solutions is required at each step of the process.

Although the strategy is named after a particular story, it actually is a method for analyzing any problem or issue with two or more sides. The steps used in this strategy are listed below.

1. Describe the situation.
   • What is the present situation?
   • What is desired?
2. What is the problem?
   • Characteristics of the pigs.
   • Characteristics of the wolf.
   • Characteristics of any other actors.
3. What changes or modifications need to be made to solve the problem?
   • What could be changed?
   • What has to be changed?
   • What are some other options?
   • What does not have to be changed?
4. Which changes would you choose, and what will be the consequences?
5. Set up an action plan to accomplish the changes.
6. State any related situations that might help in solving the problem.
7. What can we learn from those related situations that could help with this problem?

One-to-Five

This strategy combines the Big Four questions and role-playing to involve students in a discussion. By assigning various roles to students, the teacher makes each of their assignments different from the others. Not only does this provide some novelty to an in-class assignment, it also is an effective way to give students practice in group discussion and interaction.

The topic may be chosen by the teacher, or the students can choose the topic through brainstorming. The topic is then cast in the form of a public controversy.

The students are assigned to five roles in this strategy. Each role can be played by either one student or by a group of students. The roles are:

1. An expert on the topic who is preparing a table of contents for a book or article on the controversy. This student exam-

ines the topic from the perspective of what he or she feels people should know about the topic.

2. A reporter or journalist who has been assigned to the story. This student makes a list of issues from the point of view of what people want to know about the subject.

3. A person who is studying the topic. This student responds to the question, "What do I know, or think I know, about the topic?"

4. A member of the public who is curious about the topic. This player's perspective is, "What do I want to know about the topic?"

5. A member of the public who is concerned about the topic. This role represents the affective approach: "I have these feelings and beliefs, or react in the following ways, when I think about this topic."

The students are given several days to a week to prepare their roles. Students who are assigned the same role can work together to prepare for their roles. When the discussion is to begin, the students are divided into groups, with each group containing one student from each of the assigned roles.

When the teacher uses this strategy for the first time, he or she will want to structure the discussion until everyone has gained experience in using it. An example of a discussion format follows.

1. Player Five starts the discussion, which allows others to state their feelings, beliefs, and experiences.

2. Player Four tells the group what he or she wants to know about the topic.

3. Players One and Two compare their lists to see if any of their items will answer the questions of Player Four. They add any items they might have missed before reading their lists to the group and getting reactions.

4. Player Three interrupts at any time during the discussion to indicate what he or she knows or thinks is known.

The teacher who uses this strategy will find that discussions are intensive and involve much higher-level thinking, provided that the content is important and meaningful to the students. This strategy involves planning, making decisions, ordering, questioning, interacting, learning new information, identifying expertise of students, and learning how to participate in group discussions.

Little Red Riding Hood

This strategy, although a simulation, resembles actual censorship controversies. In this exercise, a group of parents and other concerned citizens are challenging the use of the story, "Little Red Riding Hood," in the school. This strategy can be especially effective if there currently is a controversy in the district, but it also can be used simply as a lead-in to discussions about censorship of any type. Students often are made aware of censorship controversies. For example, conflict over the rights of the school newspaper is a recurring issue. Starting out with a hypothetical case, the "Little Red Riding Hood" strategy can set the stage for a timely, emotionally charged exercise.

Roles for this exercise can be either assigned or offered to volunteers. One method of assigning roles is to have a group of students prepare the arguments for a role and then elect a spokesperson to represent them. The roles are:

1. The group that wants the book banned.
2. The teachers who defend its use.
3. A group of parents who support using the story.
4. The publishers of the story.
5. The president of the school board, who will make a recommendation to the board after the hearing.

To add drama, a surprise guest role can be introduced — for example, Little Red Riding Hood herself could defend her personal history.

The "hearing," which should approximate an actual school board meeting, is fascinating to watch. All of the questioning and thinking skills involved in a formal debate are in operation in this strategy, including brainstorming, research skills, organizing a case, and presentation.

I'm the Most Important

All subjects have multiple items in a number of categories. In art, for example, there are a large number of names in the category *artists*, a number of schools of art, and various media. Literature includes authors, characters, genres, and English usage as some of its components; and there are large numbers of separate items in each of those categories. A teacher can help students appreciate this by challenging them to prove that any particular item in a category is the "most important" one.

The "I'm the most important" exercise divides the class into groups and challenges each group to prove that one item is the "most important" item in a category. For example, a group of students may be asked to prove that a particular punctuation mark, such as a comma or exclamation mark, is more important than other punctuation marks. Each group is given time to marshal their arguments and then must make a presentation to the class.

This activity promotes high-level thinking skills, the use of varied resources, and creativity among students. In addition, it allows the students to achieve the same fundamental outcomes of a lesson that can be achieved with direct instruction. There is a competitive aspect to the exercise that encourages students to pay attention to the presentations of the other groups. And because the students have a stake in formulating their arguments, they are likely to learn a considerable amount about the topics and to remember the information.

The Deck of Cards

In this strategy the teacher prepares a deck of cards in which each card depicts a step in a learning process. For example, the deck may consist of a series of items about "how to study for a test." The cards are "shuffled" before they are given to the students, and the students must arrange the cards in the sequence that they prefer. This exercise encourages the students to use such thinking skills as decision making, prioritizing, sequencing, and organizing.

The questions used to begin the "deck of cards" strategy are rather general. The questions used during the debriefing stage, after the students have arranged their decks, call for the students to use many higher-level thinking skills in order to explain why they arranged the cards as they did.

Two follow-up activities can be used with this strategy. The first is to have the students apply their individual plans when studying for the next test and then to critique the results. The second activity involves higher-level thinking skills. The class is divided into groups of three, and each group is asked to reach a consensus about the proper sequence of the cards. The thinking skills involved in this strategy include: persuasion, issue resolution, problem solving, discussion skills, questioning skills, and justification, among others.

The "deck of cards" strategy is applicable to many situations in and outside of school, especially those involving planning and creating, the "how to" activities.

Commercially Available Programs

The strategies discussed above were taken from teacher workshops. There also are a number of commercially available programs and strategies for improving questioning skills. Brief overviews of those programs are provided below.

Morphological Analysis. Morphological analysis is a strategy developed by Albert Upton (1961) that can be applied to objects, actions, ideas, places, problems, and processes. It is similar to the "Idea of the Cup" exercise above in that it is a strategy to improve something that exists or that may result in a new invention. A common object, such as a stapler, can be used to demonstrate. Students are asked to list the parts of a stapler in the left-hand column of a grid, then to list its attributes or characteristics — such as size, shape, function, cost, etc. — along the top of the grid. Students are then asked to examine each cell of the grid to determine how each part or characteristic could be modified or improved. To analyze the attributes of the item, Upton uses sensory, quantitative, and qualitative categories.

Applied Imagination. In his book, *Applied Imagination* (1963), Alex Osborn advocates a unique approach to develop creativity. His method is to consider a variety of ways to think about an object, process, action, or idea by asking students to use the following types of questions to change, improve, or enlarge upon it:

- What other uses can it be put to?
- How can it be adapted to other uses?
- How can it be modified?
- What new purposes or uses would be served by magnifying it?
- What new purposes or uses could be served by "minifying" it?
- What could be substituted for it?
- How could it be rearranged to serve the purpose or use better or to serve another purpose?
- What purpose or use could it serve if the situation were reversed?
- Would new, different, or better purposes or uses be served by combining the parts in different ways?

Osborn's questions can be combined with morphological analysis.

Reciprocal Teaching. A.S. Palincsar and A.L. Brown (1985) describe reciprocal teaching as a way to develop more independence on the part of the learners. First the teacher models the procedure for reading from source material, raising questions about the material, using analytical and critiquing modes, and making predictions. The teacher then gradually turns over the process to the students. One method is to ask students to divide the source material so that one student designs questions for the first half of the assigned reading, while the other student does the same for the second half. The first student asks his or her questions of the second student, who not only answers but also raises his or her own questions about the content. The questioner then can critique the responses or ask for clarification or justification.

While the students are preparing their questions, they also must anticipate the types of questions they will be asked. This motivates them to pay attention to the learning. Eventually, they may transfer this skill to questions the teacher asks. Because students are designing their own questions, they gain a sense of direction that will lead to greater independence in studying and learning. In addition, this process allows the teacher to learn about the type and level of questions that students are designing, which may indicate the need to teach students more about designing questions that call for higher-level thinking or application.

Future Problem Solving. Future Problem Solving (Torrance and Myers 1970) is a competition that leads to the annual national Problem Solving Bowl. However, the process can be used just as effectively in individual schools, within districts, or among neighboring districts. Participating schools are given practice problems, as well as problems for the competitions. In addition, the process can be based on problems that the students identify.

There are seven steps to the Future Problem Solving process. First, students form teams and identify the components of the problem. Second, they look for the key underlying problem, the solution of which would clear up the other elements of the problem. Third, they identify as many alternatives as possible for the solution; and fourth, they develop criteria for deciding on a solution. The fifth step is to evaluate suggested alternatives using those criteria. Sixth, students design an action plan for carrying out the chosen solution. For the final step, the students must determine how to enlist the support of those who are capable of implementing the solution.

Each step requires students to address high-level questions in order to apply what they have learned to real-life situations. This method lends interest, motivation, and intensity to the study. In many cases, the solutions and action plans are presented to the decision-makers who would actually implement such a plan, for example, the school board, community governments, or legislators.

Junior Great Books. Junior Great Books is a reading program that combines outstanding literature for grades kindergarten through 12 with a questioning process to develop higher-level thinking skills. The stated philosophy of the program is:

In shared inquiry, participants learn to give full consideration to the ideas of others, to weigh the merits of opposing arguments, and to modify their initial opinions as the evidence demands. They gain experience in communicating complex ideas and in supporting, testing, and expanding their own thoughts. In this way, the shared inquiry method promotes thoughtful dialogue and open debate, preparing its participants to become able, responsible citizens, as well as enthusiastic, lifelong readers. (Junior Great Books 1992)

The Junior Great Books selections are measurably better than those found in most basal reading series. A two-day leadership training program is mandatory to participate in the program. Leaders are chosen from a variety of backgrounds and disciplines.

SCAMPER. SCAMPER is a creative-questioning program developed by Robert F. Eberle (1971). It was based originally on stories that were used to promote creativity and drew from the work of Torrance and Osborn. Osborn's book, *Applied Imagination* (1963), describes the process more fully. SCAMPER stands for types of questions:

Substitute: What can serve in place of another?
Combine: What can be combined to bring together disparate elements, or to make a better product or outcome?
Modify, magnify, or minify: How can something be changed in form or quality, or put to new uses?
Put to other uses: What other purposes can the object serve?
Eliminate: What positive results can be realized by eliminating some nonessentials?
Reverse, rearrange: What can be accomplished by changing the order of the original process?

Jeopardy. Another approach to questioning is to use the format of the television program, "Jeopardy," in which answers are provided and students match them with questions.

There are many other commercial programs on the market that purport to improve questioning skills of teachers and students.

Information about new programs for improving questioning skills can be obtained at conferences on curriculum development, such as those held by the Association for Supervision and Curriculum Development, Phi Delta Kappa International, and the National Association of Gifted Children, or through special workshops.

CHAPTER FIVE

Shaping the Question-Response Transaction

Once the objectives for the questions have been set and the particular questioning strategies have been chosen, teachers need to consider five elements before they actually ask the questions. The following elements are necessary aspects for preparing effective questions:

1. The wording of the question should indicate the type of thinking required of students and the way in which the content will be used or applied.
2. The question should attend to the conditions that influence whether students decide to respond.
3. The question should attend to the conditions that influence the content of student responses.
4. The question should attend to the conditions that affect the accuracy and quality of student responses.
5. The teacher must anticipate the likely or possible responses of students and must prepare to react to student responses in order to encourage participation.

Teachers need to make it possible for students to respond to a question. To do that, teachers need to make it clear to students just what the question calls for. Teachers also need to make sure that students have the background knowledge in order to respond to the question. They need to anticipate the possible student responses in order to prepare activities that will allow the question to lead to higher-level thinking.

Response Clues

The wording of a question provides students with clues to the appropriate response. The teacher should let students know what is expected of them. For example, if the teacher states, "Here is a question that I would like you to discuss," the students know that the response is open-ended and that they are to share their ideas. If a particular type of thinking is required, then the question should indicate that explicitly by using such words as "analyze," "summarize," or "interpret," rather than just asking students to "think about" the material.

It is important to ensure that students understand what the teacher is asking for in a question. Thus, when a teacher first asks students to "analyze" or "summarize" something, the teacher might ask students to define those words. In that way, the entire class will be able to approach the question with the same level of understanding.

Student Decisions to Respond

Once a question has been asked, the power in the classroom shifts to the students. The students determine what happens next. The first decision that students will make is whether to respond to the question and to become actively involved in the discussion.

There are two sets of conditions that influence a student's decision to respond to a question. The first set concerns the student's knowledge, experiences, and ideas. Those conditions determine the student's perception of his or her ability to respond to the question. The second set of conditions concerns the student's attitudes, that is, whether the student wants to respond.

When a student decides whether he or she is able to respond to the question, one of the first questions the student will consider is whether he or she knows the answer. If the question has a single, correct answer, the decision to respond will depend on the student's memory.

While a question that requires a single, correct answer will eliminate the need for other students to become involved in that question, such recitation questions can be used to involve students in the questions that follow. A teacher can ask just enough recitation questions to help students recall enough information to engage in higher levels of thinking. In that way, students will be more able to respond to the questions that call for such higher-level thinking.

When the question requires open-ended responses, higher-level thinking, or input based on students' experiences, students will ask themselves other questions to determine if they are able to respond. Some of the questions students will ask themselves are:

- What does the question ask me to do? What does it mean?
- What do I need to know in order to respond?
- What kind of thinking is expected?
- Am I good at that type of thinking?
- Does the question require me to make use of or apply course material?
- Can I think of applications or uses for the content?
- What do I know, or think I know? What do I remember?
- Does the question ask me to make an interpretation, draw a conclusion, make a generalization?
- Can I support my response?

The students' attitudes or dispositions also determine whether they will contribute to the class. Students should want to respond and feel comfortable enough to risk responding to questions.

Before a student decides whether he or she wants to respond to a question, the student will mentally ask, "Is this important to me?" Teachers might not like to think that this should be a consideration for students, but understanding the material's relevance to career or personal goals is important in a student's decision to participate. Teachers must consider this factor before they ask their questions; they should plan to demonstrate the relevance of a subject when they plan the lesson.

Past classroom experiences have a great impact on students' decisions to become involved in class discussions. These past experiences will provide the answers to other questions that students might ask before they decide to contribute to a class:

- Do I know how to respond in an acceptable manner?
- Can I express myself well?
- If I respond, how will my response be treated?

The answers to these questions are very important to students. Unless their previous responses — which might have contained errors — and their expressed opinions are met with courtesy, understanding, and positive actions by teachers, it is unlikely that students will choose to respond. They also are unlikely to respond if they see their classmates treated poorly after they have risked a response to a teacher's question.

Certainly, a teacher should use questioning to help students explore their misconceptions and even their prejudices. But it is essential for the teacher to be open and nonjudgmental when students initially respond. It is important for the teacher to express a willingness to try to understand the reasoning behind every student response. Otherwise, students' inclination to participate will be diminished.

There are some general aspects of the classroom that can affect a student's willingness to participate. Some common aspects that deter or promote participation are discussed below.

Atmosphere as a Deterrent. A positive, open, humane atmosphere is necessary for and conducive to student participation. Immature responses by teachers, such as the use of sarcasm and other negative statements, will stop classroom interactions not only for the student who is the object of the negative statement, but also for those who may be concerned that they will be treated similarly.

Interestingly, teacher responses that on the surface might seem positive can have unintended effects on students. In open-ended interactions, agreeing with a student is an evaluative device that may dissuade other students who had considered offering different views or ideas, because they feel that the prior response must be the right one or the one the teacher wanted. Furthermore, simply agreeing with a statement does not inspire the student to think about it.

Praise as a Deterrent. Even praise can discourage involvement. Except when used to promote positive behavior or to encourage students with emotional needs, praise by itself puts a stop to interaction. For example, when a teacher says to a student, "That was a fine report," the student can say little except, "Thank you." That ends the discussion.

When a teacher praises a student's response, that also can end discussion. Other students may interpret that praise as indicating that the teacher received the one "correct" answer.

In order to be effective, praise should include concrete reasons for the praise. Praise also can be effective with individual students in such feedback situations as comments on tests, reports, and writing assignments or in conferences. However, teachers should be very selective in using praise during questioning.

Leading Questions as Deterrents. There is a difference between phrasing questions so students know what type of thinking is required and using leading words or phrases that limit the variety of responses that students can make. Questions that include leading words confine students' thinking and, therefore, their contributions. Some examples follow:

Leading Questions	**Impartial Questions**
Tell me what you *liked* about the story.	How do you feel about the story?
Why was this a *good* poem?	What is your reaction to the poem?
Why were his actions *right*?	
Explain why Bill's ideas were *better.*	What were the consequences of his actions?
Tell why the United States *should have* taken that action.	Whose ideas were better?
	Should the U.S. have taken that action?

Leading words limit the acceptable responses. When faced with such questions, students may choose not to contribute or, worse, give the answer they think the teacher will find acceptable. This denies the opportunity for the teacher and the class to learn divergent ideas.

Showing Interest. While simple praise can sometimes act as a deterrent to classroom participation, statements or questions that demonstrate interest in students' responses will promote participation. Showing interest entails asking for more information about a student's ideas and also asking questions to find out more about the student. The teacher also gains from the interaction by learning something new about the student and his or her thought processes.

The Content of Student Responses

The responses that students give to a question are not always those for which a teacher planned. Indeed, student responses sometimes will present problems for the teacher's plan. Teachers need to anticipate all the possible student responses in order to prepare activities and questions that will allow the lesson to continue.

There are at least eight factors that affect the content of student responses. Each factor will determine the options that the teacher has for dealing with a student's response. The eight factors that typically influence the content of a student's response are:

1. Sometimes students have dealt with a situation in real life that is inconsistent with the way it is presented in the text or resource materials. The teacher's questioning strategy here is to reconcile the two or to explore them further to determine if one is more valid.
2. Student responses may be based on beliefs, feelings, biases, prejudices, or values that were instilled in their homes or formed by their religious backgrounds, peer-group norms, or other social and family factors.
3. Student responses may be based on their past successes or failures in school.

4. The students' age will influence their thinking and attitudes.
5. What students have learned previously, both in and out of
school, may make them reluctant to consider other possibilities.
6. Students' cultural backgrounds may affect their responses.
7. Exposure to propaganda that appeals to students' personal or group beliefs may affect their responses.
8. Students' past experiences in similar situations will affect
their responses.

These influences are very important to students. Teachers must
try to understand the factors that have influenced a student's response and recognize the implications of those factors. Once
teachers have achieved this understanding, they can go beyond
what the student has said to explore the response further.

The Accuracy and Quality of Student Responses

A variety of conditions affect the accuracy and quality of students' responses. Some of these factors will be operating during
any lesson, so teachers need to take them into account when planning a lesson and designing questions.

One common factor that affects student responses is how recently the student learned the material. When a student answers
incorrectly, it is not uncommon for the teacher to say, "Didn't you
learn that last year?" or "Don't you recall that from when we
studied that earlier this year?" Student time is different than adult
time. One year for a six-year-old is one-sixth of his or her life.
The three-year interval from seventh to tenth grade represents
one-fifth of a student's life.

The teacher must use questioning strategies that help students
retrieve prior knowledge or treat it as though it is new information. Accordingly, when discussing information that was not
learned very recently, it often is more productive for questions to
call for such "big ideas" as concepts, generalizations, laws, or
principles, rather than emphasizing specific facts.

Another condition affecting the quality of students' responses is how often they have needed or used the information since they initially learned it. When students use information frequently, they retain it. When students have had little or no need for the past learning, it becomes difficult to retrieve.

Students' interest and motivation also affect their learning. Students' interests vary, and a lack of interest often may be attributed to the material's lack of relevance to them. The questions a teacher chooses must focus on helping students relate the learning to their past, present, or future lives. In addition, teachers must use alternative strategies to increase students' interest. Students must see ways in which the learning is useful.

The depth of prior learning also affects students' ability to respond accurately and meaningfully. There are many instructional aspects that determine how well learning is retained. These include how much the teacher emphasized concepts, generalizations, laws, and principles, rather than just facts, and how often students have opportunities to use the material after it was learned.

Sometimes students are unable to retrieve information efficiently in order to respond appropriately. When the teacher uses a series of refocusing questions, which draw out basic information, students are able to retrieve the material.

Students' mastery of prerequisite knowledge and skills also influences their preparedness for new material. It is the teacher's responsibility to identify the knowledge and skills that students need to benefit from new material. Pretests in the skill areas and presurveys in the content areas will help teachers determine the knowledge and skills that need to be developed.

The accuracy of a student's response also can be affected by irregular attendance and lack of attention in class. Teachers can not control whether a student attends school. However, the degree to which a teacher employs recognized motivational strategies, such as novelty, variety, and relevance, will increase or decrease students' attentiveness. Teachers' enthusiasm about a subject and their devotion to upgrading their knowledge and teaching skills also are factors in student motivation.

Reacting to Student Responses

The next action returns the initiative to the teacher. The student has responded, and now the teacher decides what kind of interaction to pursue. The teacher can stop the interaction with a simple "Thank you," which acknowledges the response and praises the student. Other interaction stoppers are disparagement of the student's response, which will discourage other students from responding ("Am I the next to be embarrassed?"), or a comment such as, "That's the best response," which signals that other students need not try to top it.

To continue positive interaction, the teacher can choose among several strategies, such as asking questions that call for elaboration or clarification, actively listening, playing devil's advocate, using deliberate silence, responding with a personal viewpoint, or simply showing interest.

When planning their questions, teachers need to prepare for students' possible responses to each question. Their reaction to a student's response will determine whether the interaction will continue. An inappropriate reaction will end the discussion and stymie further thinking, but a well-planned response will ensure the kind of interaction that promotes further discussion and higher-level thinking.

Following are some of the categories into which student responses might fall. These are followed by suggested starter questions that the teacher can use to promote further discussion.

1. Supportable or insupportable responses. Many student responses either can or cannot be supported by the information in the response. In this case, the teacher must ask the student to validate or corroborate the response by asking for examples, references, or other support material. The teacher also might ask the rest of the class for their opinions about the response or to compare it with their experiences. Some questions the teacher can use for this type of response are:

- Where did you find that information?
- Where did you get that idea?

- Whose idea was it originally?
- What support do you have for that?

2. Students' opinions, feelings, beliefs, ideas, or positions. Again, it is appropriate to ask students to support their statements, for example:

- What or who led you to feel or believe that?
- How long have you believed that?
- Are there any reasons that would cause you to change your feeling or belief?
- Do others that you know feel or believe the same? Differently?
- What would cause others to believe that or feel the same way?
- Would your opinion be the same if (propose a different situation)?
- Here are some objections that I have heard to that opinion. How would you respond to these?
- I am going to restate what you have said. Is this accurate?
- What assumptions are you making?
- How does your feeling or belief fit in with (provide counter-example)?
- How does that feeling or belief affect your life?

3. Responses based on students' experiences. When the student's response is based on personal experiences, the teacher's questions should enable the student to compare his or her experiences with others' in the same situation to see how their experiences might be the same or different. Some examples of such teacher questions are:

- How many times has this occurred?
- Give some examples.
- Where, or with whom, did this occur?
- What are the consequences of having had that experience?
- Have other people you know had that experience?
- How have you handled other experiences that were unlike that one?

- How is your experience similar to or different from the situation described?
- What conditions might have changed your experience or its outcome?

4. Predictions or hypotheses. The types of question that are appropriate in these cases will establish criteria to determine the accuracy and validity of the responses, whether they meet acceptable standards. The teacher's questions might include:

- What information enabled you to make that prediction?
- What assumptions are you making?
- What or who is the source of your information?
- What conditions have to exist for the prediction to come true?
- What would be some consequences if your prediction came true?
- What conditions or circumstances could happen that would change your prediction?
- If the prediction should be changed, what could an individual or group do to change it?
- How could we set up a situation to test it?
- What are the pros and cons of your predicted result?

5. Responses in the form of questions. If students' questions focus on procedural matters, the teacher must find out if the instructions for the assignment were incomplete or unclear. If their questions indicate confusion, lack of understanding, or perplexity, the teacher needs to encourage students to clarify their areas of confusion. The teacher should ask the student the reasons for his or her question to ensure that it is answered accurately. Some examples are:

- Tell me more about your question.
- What caused you to raise the question?
- What don't you understand?
- What do you mean by. . . ?
- Do you mean. . . ?

Sometimes when students' responses include another question, the subject of the question has to do with something other than the material in the lesson. For example, if students consistently seek the teacher's permission or approval when responding (Is this all right? Is this what you wanted?), it might be because the classroom atmosphere is restrictive or requires them to conform. The teacher must investigate that situation. The student also might be demonstrating dependency. In that case, the teacher, without giving approval or evaluation, should lead the student to answer his or her own question.

6. Responses in the form of analogies. This is a more complex type of student response. Questions that help them understand the similarities and differences between the real situation and the analogy are important not only to demonstrate the value of the analogy to understanding, but also to develop the difference between the two to show that they are not interchangeable. Examples of questions the teacher might ask are:

- What made you think about that as an analogy?
- In what ways is the analogy like the situation, action, or idea?
- In what ways is it different?
- Explain how the analogy helps you to understand the situation, action, or idea?

7. Vague responses. The teacher's questions should prompt the student to provide more concrete details, explanation, or examples that will clarify the student's response. For example:

- Explain what you mean by that.
- What is the basis for that response? How many examples can you give?
- Here is another example of the situation. How does that fit in with your statement?
- How could we test your statement? How often does it happen?

8. Generalizations. A generalization usually has a sufficient number of cases to support it. However, students' generalizations often do not. Teachers' questions must help the students understand when they have enough data or examples for their responses to qualify as a generalization.

9. Biased or prejudicial responses. When a student's response uses stereotypes, the teacher's questions can help the student identify the propaganda that has promoted that stereotype. The teacher's questions should encourage students to analyze the situation and separate the individual person, situation, or action from the group with which it is being associated. For example:

- How do stereotypes develop?
- Why do you think this characteristic is typical of that person, group, or situation?
- Give some examples or experiences that support your response.
- Have you had many interactions with the people in this group?
- Can you think of any examples that go against that stereotype?
- What would it take to change your point of view?
- In the next two weeks, make a list of all the situations that support your point of view.

10. Misdirected responses. The student might have mistakenly responded to a different question. Obviously, questions that redirect the student's thinking are appropriate in this case:

- If I had asked you _____, your answer would be appropriate. However, the question was _____.

11. The "I-don't-know" response. The techniques for dealing with this response were discussed in Chapter 2.

12. Responses that students' think the teacher wants to hear. Students sometimes will tailor their responses so that they match what they believe the teacher expects. In these cases, the teacher should ask the student:

- Is that what you really believe?

13. Responses based on emotion. In these cases, the teacher's questions must be designed carefully so that they do not intimidate the student. When the teacher cannot design a question that will not intimidate a particular student, the teacher should direct the question to the entire class to avoid focusing on the individual student. Some questions that will not intimidate the student are:

- Is this an accurate statement of what you were saying? (paraphrase)
- It seems that you feel strongly about this. How do those feelings affect your actions?
- What experiences have you had that made you feel so strongly about this?
- Why do people feel strongly about things? Why not?
- What positive actions can be taken because of your feelings?
- What negative results might occur?
- What can be done to cause people to explore their strong emotions?

14. The student refuses to accept information that contradicts or refutes his or her response. Many people adopt this position at some time in their lives. This should be considered a problem only if a student exhibits this conduct consistently. While questioning strategies may help the student recognize and deal with this position, the situation may call for counseling to determine why the student refuses to change in the light of valid information. Some questions the teacher might use in this situation are:

- Let's suppose you are right. What are the consequences, outcomes, results of that thinking?
- Let's think about this in another way. Suppose. . . .
- How would you feel if. . . ? (Give counter-examples, state different positions, or assign a different role.)
- Let's suppose I felt that you were right (or wrong). What questions would you ask me?
- List your reasons for your position.

- How does that position affect your daily life?
- Here's a scenario. React to it from your position.

15. Evaluations or judgments. When the student's response is an evaluation or judgment, the teacher's questions must call for the student to demonstrate his or her reasoning.

- What criteria or standards did you use in making your evaluation?
- Here are some other criteria. Would they affect your evaluation? How?
- If your evaluation is valid, what would strengthen the negative parts? Overcome the missing elements? Improve the object of the evaluation?
- How will your evaluation affect your future actions or decisions?
- In what ways could you improve your evaluation abilities?

16. Interpretations or conclusions. When the student has been called on to make an interpretation or draw a conclusion, the teacher's questions should ask the student to give some justification for his or her response and to explain the processes the student used to reach his or her conclusion.

- What are the various factors or elements that affected your interpretation or conclusion?
- What data do you have to support your conclusion?
- Explain the process that you went through in arriving at that conclusion.
- What do you predict would happen as a result of your conclusion?
- How could your conclusion be tested?
- What are the consequences if your conclusion is valid?

17. Controversial responses. A student's response may be based on one side of a controversy, or two students may argue for different sides of a controversy. The teacher's follow-up questions should seek to reveal the areas where both sides can agree and those where there is extreme disagreement. The questions should be similar to those used in conflict resolution.

- What are the causes of the controversy?
- What are the different positions?
- What will you use to defend your position?
- Your assignment is to defend each other's positions.
- What are some areas of agreement?
- State those positions that you feel that you cannot change, and list your reasons.
- Evaluate each aspect of the other positions.

18. Creative or original responses. When a student presents a creative or original response, the teacher's follow-up questions should help the entire class understand the thinking processes that went into the response. These questions will call for clarification, elaboration, and an examination of the consequences of the idea and how it could be developed further.

19. Incorrect responses. Sometimes a student's response will be either partially or totally wrong. The teacher's questioning strategy must lead the student through the steps to overcome the error.

These 19 categories of possible responses can be applied to most open-ended class discussions. By anticipating student responses, the teacher can plan follow-up questions and other exploratory strategies so that the students will achieve the objectives and outcomes of the lesson. The teacher should be able to turn any student response into an opportunity to further thinking skills and applications of the learning.

A Final Question

Teachers need to ask themselves: What will I do to improve my students' questioning skills?

Students need to be aware that questions fall into two major categories: those that call for memory and those that call for some type of thought. By acquainting students with the preceding list and giving them opportunities to practice, teachers can help students understand how certain types of questions stimulate higher-order thinking.

One useful strategy is to take teacher- or student-designed questions, identify their type, and practice making them into higher-order questions. Other strategies include:

- Use open-ended questions to generate group brainstorming.
- Ask students to write their responses before answering verbally.
- Have students rewrite their answers following a class discussion.
- Give students opportunities to critique one another's answers.

Finally, it often is helpful to move students beyond "I don't know" by taking the specific to the more general. Students may respond with "I don't know" about the Civil War, but all students have experienced conflict. So take the discussion to the general and talk about conflict — then bring it back to the specific, the Civil War. Instead of AIDS, focus on disease; instead of elections, focus on making choices; and so forth. Simple changes can redirect students' thinking, and such redirection can help students better understand the power of questions to evoke thinking.

CHAPTER SIX

Improving Assessment, Evaluation, and Testing with Better Questioning

Assessment is essential. Teachers use assessment to evaluate their effectiveness and as a guide to planning. Properly used, assessments allow students to measure their comprehension of current material and to better prepare for subsequent learning. Assessment also is essential to parents, administrators, and school boards in evaluating teaching and learning. Schools need definite measures to monitor their programs.

A dilemma arises when assessments focus on students' memorization abilities, rather than on what they know and what they can do. Teachers are concerned that, by infusing more higher-level thinking and questioning into instruction, they will lack time to teach factual information or to cover enough text material so that students score well on standardized tests.

There are efforts at the state and national levels to develop standardized tests that assess higher-level thinking and applications of content. However, there is a difference between using higher-level questions in class and including them on tests. Students' written responses on a test constitute only the products of their thinking, not their strategies or reasoning. In the classroom, teachers immediately can ask questions about processes or reasons. Accomplishing that with a written test is difficult and time-consuming.

This chapter will focus on teacher-made evaluation strategies. When teachers use their own assessment strategies, they have complete control over the content and method to be used, as well as what will be evaluated.

The terms assessment, evaluation, and testing often are used interchangeably. In this book, assessment is the broadest of the three and encompasses the purposes, methods, and forms of learning. Evaluation is an assessment that is done to assign a rating, grade, or value to a student's work. Testing is the instrument chosen for an assessment.

Purposes of Assessment

Every assessment should be viewed as an extension of the unit of learning. It should be designed to help students achieve the intended goals for the unit. Students should be able to learn from the assessment, not only about the material of the subject but also about how to learn efficiently, how to prepare for tests, and how to apply learning.

Assessments serve various purposes. At the beginning of a school year or before a unit of study, they can be used to determine student weaknesses and strengths. Assessments that follow a unit might accomplish the following:

- Identify student progress and achievement, either in skill development or processing ability.
- Determine students' abilities to apply content or new thinking skills to other situations.
- Determine grades or other ratings.
- Determine teacher effectiveness in planning, instruction, and evaluation and aid in future planning.

Evaluations also are important for purposes outside the classroom. Evaluations give parents some idea of their child's progress and success; they provide a basis for discussions with the child and the teacher. Evaluations are needed for reports to administrators and school boards on the success of students and the effectiveness of instruction. They also provide a means for parents and taxpayers to ascertain a district's accountability.

When preparing an evaluation, the teacher first needs to decide the purpose it will serve. The evaluation should complement the questioning strategy that the teacher used in the unit. Thus the teacher must consider these questions:

- Will it test the essential facts and information of the unit?
- Will it evaluate students' ability to apply their learning?
- Will it challenge their thinking about the learning?
- What proportion of the test will be allotted to each purpose?
- Will it be an isolated measure of students' achievement or will it measure their progress from a previous assessment?

The purposes for the evaluation should be written in objective or outcome-based terminology. These outcome statements should denote the "big ideas" of the unit, the concepts, generalizations, laws, principles, ideas, thinking skills, and content applications. The individual test questions should be designed to meet these outcome statements. And the questioning strategy should allow for a variety of solutions, resolutions, decisions, and ideas in order to cause students to think. That will ensure that the evaluation does more than just test for facts but also contributes to the learning of those larger ideas.

The teacher should design the questions for the test at the beginning of the unit, at the same time as the classroom questions are designed. This will enable the teacher to use the evaluation as a focus when planning the lessons. This approach also allows the teacher to design practice activities that will prepare students for the type of thinking or applications they will need in the test.

The students can be made aware at the start of the unit about how to organize their learning to prepare for the test. When students know the expected outcomes, they can develop their own strategies to achieve them. In addition, students will be better able to ask questions that will increase their proficiency not only on the particular test, but also for many other types of evaluation.

Improving Test Results

Sometimes it is difficult to determine if a student scored poorly on a test because the student did not know enough of the content or because he or she did not know how to take a particular type of test. Thus the teacher needs to prepare students for the particular method of evaluation and to devote time to teaching test-taking skills. And teachers should observe students during a test or in debriefing sessions afterward in order to identify what test-taking skills they need.

At the start of a new unit, students should be told how they will be evaluated, that is, what kind of a test they will receive at the end of the unit. Preparation for objective tests, essay tests, and application tests require different approaches during the learning process. Knowledge about the type of test at the start of a unit enables students to adjust their thinking and study as the learning progresses, rather than having to make last-minute adjustments preparing for the test.

Students should be taught specific strategies for taking different types of tests — that is, true-false, multiple choice, matching, and essay — and practice in these skills and strategies should be provided often. For example, on true-false tests, students should be taught to mark false any item that is partially wrong. Two techniques that give students an advantage on multiple-choice tests are:

1. Rule out two options, then concentrate on the other two.
2. Think of an answer before looking at the options.

Students can practice with long multiple-choice items to determine with which approach they feel more comfortable, reading the item and then the options, or reading the options and then the item.

When students are to be given matching tests, they should be shown ways to use the process of elimination. Looking for key words in the left column that are synonymous to key words in the right column is one strategy that often is helpful on standardized, commercial tests, as well as on teacher-designed tests.

Robert Blackey (1988) suggests that teachers also should give their students comprehensive training for answering essay questions. That training should include practice sessions, use of student writing models, and opportunities to rewrite after critique. The practice sessions should include training in writing the thematic introduction, the body of supporting evidence, and the conclusion.

When practicing with essay questions, students should ask themselves such questions as, "What points will I make because of the thinking that I am asked to do in the question?" and "What will be included in my summary or conclusion?" Students should learn to outline their responses before they write their essay.

Practicing strategies for standardized tests is essential if the test formats differ from those designed by the teacher. This practice should include the manner in which the students will be asked to write their answers, for example, on the test sheet or on a separate "bubble sheet."

There are several techniques that students can use to prepare for any test:

- Read the entire test before you start.
- Learn how to allot time on the test.
- Carefully listen to or read the directions for the various parts of a test.
- Skip the most difficult questions until you have answered the other questions.
- In math tests, use estimation.

The following guidelines will help teachers prepare their tests so that the test will allow students to perform at their optimal levels:

- Write test questions at the start of the unit to provide direction to the instruction.
- Make sure the test directions are clear and complete.
- Write the answers to open-ended questions as standards for evaluation.

- Determine how much of each test will focus on various areas and types of questions.
- Avoid using extreme words, such as "always" and "never."
- Use correct grammar, spelling, and punctuation.
- Establish a comfortable atmosphere.

Test Design

Entire books are devoted to test construction. This discussion will be restricted to some broad guidelines for constructing tests and how test questions can encourage higher-level thinking.

The first guideline is for the teacher to determine the purpose for an evaluation. The purpose will determine the types of questions that are used in a test. To evaluate knowledge acquisition or retention, traditional tests are suitable. To evaluate skill development, the test should require students to demonstrate or perform the skill. If attitudinal changes are the objective, pre- and postsurveys should be designed. If students' products and performances are to be evaluated, criteria should be established when the assignment is made. Evaluation of students' abilities to demonstrate a process also should be based on established criteria and anticipated outcomes. Thinking-skill competencies call for parallel test situations to be given periodically so that progress can be determined. Abilities to apply content material can be based on given situations, such as scenarios, case studies, or simulations.

When the purpose of the test is to determine how well students have acquired knowledge of facts, evaluations still can incorporate questions that promote higher-level thinking. The questions on such a test should ask students to think about facts in different ways. For example:

- Who determines that something is a fact, or how does something become accepted as a fact?
- What caused it to come into being? What need did it serve?
- What could change or eliminate its status as a fact?
- Can you give examples of something that was but no longer is a fact?

- What is the consequence or value of this fact? What are its implications?
- Can you think of examples of facts that have been proven wrong but still are believed by a significant number of people?
- How can we tell the difference between a fact, belief, and superstition?
- How does somebody get credit for a discovery, invention, data, process, or idea?
- Give examples of people who were laughed at or punished for stating what later proved to be a fact.

Analyzing facts in this way will give the students an appreciation of what is involved in the classification of something as fact. It will help them become more skilled at examining information presented as fact. Eventually such strategies should become automatic in students' learning activities, whether they are initiated by the school or the students themselves. These types of questions can promote a healthy skepticism by posing the question, "So what?" about the importance, validity, and implications of any fact-based learning.

There are a number of types of questions that are common among traditional, paper-and-pencil tests. These include true-false, multiple choice, completion, matching, and essay questions. Regardless of the type of test, all items of the same type should be on the same page so that students do not have to flip pages to complete a section. Below are some specific guidelines for designing these questions.

True-False. Three practices to avoid in true-false tests are: using such extreme words as "always" and "never," making the "true" or best answer the longest answer, and organizing questions to create an identifiable pattern of T's or F's. Experts disagree whether "all of the above" or "none of the above" should be options, since these options can be misleading.

True-false questions can be transformed easily into higher-level questions. Instead of using single statements, the test can include scenarios, essays, situations, editorials, or descriptive passages. The students must choose which following statement is the best analysis, which indicates the most likely trend, which best expresses the main idea of the writing, or which is the most likely prediction.

Multiple Choice. Multiple-choice items usually require students to choose the correct or best answer, typically from four selections. In addition to the correct answer, there usually is a distracter — an item that is close but not correct.

Multiple-choice test items can be transformed into higher-level questions by describing scenarios, situations, case studies, or problems and providing alternatives for the main ideas, probable outcomes, or best solutions. The questions can ask which concepts, conclusions, or generalizations can be drawn from the selection or which laws or principles are involved. In some cases, students can be asked to write justifications for their choices.

Each of the following question formats can be converted into higher-level questions in a similar manner.

Completion. When the test questions call for students to fill in a blank, teachers need to decide whether to supply the domain of answers or to have students rely on memory for the answers. If the possible answers are listed on the test, there should be more alternatives listed than are necessary. Otherwise, items should be allowed to be used for more than one question. Whichever alternative is chosen, the statements must be worded so that only one response is correct.

Matching. Matching tests should be confined to eight to twelve items that are in the same category. Matching tests that mix categories (for example, people and events, objects and ideas, processes and persons) are "giveaways" for students and do not evaluate their knowledge. One strategy is to have the right column contain more alternatives than are in the left or to provide more than one match for an item.

Essays. An effective essay question can be one of the most challenging test questions for a teacher to write. Without indicating what the students are to do with the knowledge needed to answer the question, an essay test becomes merely another way to demonstrate knowledge of facts. An essay question is not properly graded on the number of facts students provide, but on what the question asked them to do with those facts.

Essay questions should require students to do something with their knowledge. For example, students can be asked to analyze the significance of something, to rank the importance of items and justify their ranking, to indicate trends, to predict consequences, or to interpret the meaning of items. Whatever specific task is required, all essay questions should require students to support their responses. In addition, the instructions for each question should state explicitly what the student is required to do.

There are several variations on essay tests that require students to go beyond facts to apply their knowledge and use other higher-level thinking skills. For example, open-book tests can be used when detailed or comprehensive information already is located in one or more of the resources used during the study. Because students are able to look up the facts during the test, the questions in an open-book test will allow students to concentrate on using higher-level thinking skills.

Another variation on the essay test is to present students with a list of the terms or concepts involved in a unit of study. The students must classify or categorize these items and provide reasons for their decisions.

Robert Blackey (1988) suggests that essay tests offer multiple questions so that students can chose to respond to the questions for which they are best prepared. Blackey also suggests that time be given during the test for students to formulate ideas, to organize an approach, and to proofread their responses for both mechanical errors and content.

Alternative Assessment Strategies

Alternative assessment strategies go beyond traditional types of testing. While some require pencil and paper, most often they consist of student performances, projects, demonstrations, or portfolio presentations. These assessments are meant to approximate situations that students will encounter out of school, hence the term authentic assessment.

Performances, processes, and products already are used for assessments in the fine arts, the practical arts, technology, and physical education, as well as in composition, speech, foreign language, and mathematics. It is for the other content areas that alternative assessments must be developed.

There are three important questions to be answered in designing authentic assessments:

- What major learning and understanding should be assessed?
- How can the study be transformed or translated into tasks or activities that simulate real-life situations in which students will be involved?
- What criteria will need to be developed to accurately evaluate the students' performances, products, and methods?

In order to make an assessment "authentic," teachers need to consider how the assessment will increase student competency in a thinking skill through practice, increase student competencies in skills unique to the subject, and approximate what is expected of students in real-life situations.

In order to design assessments that approximate what is expected in real-life situations, teachers first need to answer the following questions:

- What do geographers, historians, etc., study in their daily work? How do they operate?
- What applied mathematics do many people use in their daily work and personal lives?
- How do writers and artists get their ideas and develop them?
- How do scientists identify, study, and solve problems?
- How do office managers plan new systems and methods to increase efficiency?
- How do people get ideas for and design games and the rules of play?
- How do engineers adapt the work of scientists to practical use?

Answers to these questions can be found in encyclopedias or texts devoted to the disciplines; and many of the tasks are identified in the SCANS report from 1992. However, perhaps the best way to answer these questions is to have the students interview people in a variety of careers. These interviews will ensure that the students recognize the relationship between the school-based assignment and the work place. Being able to demonstrate that an assignment is related to what students will have to do in the future is very useful for answering the familiar question, "Why do we have to do this?"

Authentic assessments can take many forms. Some examples of assessment activities are:

- Design or make a construction that demonstrates a law, principle, or idea.
- Invent a device to solve a problem or to improve a process or product.
- Write editorials, letters to the editor, or essays about a controversy and submit them to a newspaper.
- Maintain a journal of reactions to literature or issues studied.
- Create an audiovisual production that is creative or that conveys a particular situation or idea.
- Conduct an oral history.
- Participate in a debate.
- Conduct a case study.
- Conduct an experiment to test a hypothesis.

Authentic assessments require three conditions in order to be effective. First, the criteria that will be used to evaluate the assessments must be set at the time an assignment is made. Setting criteria at the start of an assignment provides a measure for students as they prepare their assigned product or performance. When students do not know the criteria by which their work will be judged, even the most conscientious students are put in a position of having to guess how the teacher will evaluate their work.

When students know in advance the criteria for judging their work, the typical student question changes from "I wonder what

grade the teacher will give me?" to "I wonder how my evaluation
of my work and the teacher's evaluation will agree?" When only
grades are given, teacher-student discussion usually focuses solely
on the reason for the grade. Making students aware of the criteria
allows teacher-student discussion to focus on the instructional
aspects of the evaluation.

As students gain more experience with authentic assessments,
they also should be given a role in setting the criteria by which
their products will be evaluated. This improves students' self-
evaluation skills.

One popular form of criterion is the rubric. A rubric is a series
of three to six levels of descriptive statements that are applied to
the student's performance or product for evaluation. They can be
written in a variety of ways, such as acceptable to unacceptable
or minimal to optimal competency. Examples of rubrics are
included in *Assessing Student Outcomes: Performance Assessment Using the Dimensions of Learning* (Marzano, Pickering,
and McTighe 1993).

A common problem is that students often focus on the question,
"Will this be on the test?" This arises from an emphasis on grades
and from tests based on a student's ability to memorize. When the
emphasis of the test is changed from facts to higher-level thinking
and application, the student's question becomes, "Will we have
these types of situations on the test?" However, even though a
teacher may have designed learning activities that require higher-
level thinking and application, using those same activities on the
test will again measure only the student's memory.

Evaluating Thinking Skills

Not every student's complete repertoire of thinking skills can
be evaluated each year by each teacher. However, teachers do
need to determine if their students need to improve their thinking
skills. One strategy is that each teacher in a school, or all the
teachers in a department or school, chooses four to eight thinking
skills to emphasize during the year. The teachers then design
questions that focus on the selected skills.

The teachers then should design tests that evaluate the selected thinking skills. These tests should be used first at the beginning of the year in order to provide baseline data — for both individual students and the class — about students' thinking skills. This data will enable teachers to determine what skills need to be developed further. The students should be given practice sessions in these skills, with further evaluations conducted two or three more times during the year. Each evaluation should be used to document the growth in students' thinking skills and to plan new instruction.

For example, if the teacher has decided to emphasize the thinking skill of comparing and contrasting, the first step would be to develop a test to evaluate the students' use of that skill. Students could be asked to compare and contrast two or more people, things, or places with which they are familiar. Their responses would be evaluated according to four criteria: quantity, variety (indicating they have analyzed the comparisons from many different viewpoints), the maturity or sophistication of the responses, and originality or creativity.

When diagnosing students' abilities to compare, teachers should ask open-ended questions in order to reveal students' current skills and approaches. However, when conducting an evaluation, the questions should focus students' attention on specific aspects to compare. By limiting the possible responses, the teacher reduces the variables to be evaluated.

The questions used in these evaluations should have two purposes: to encourage students to employ that particular type of thinking during the evaluation and to help them to develop that thinking skill through discussions and setting criteria during the practice sessions.

It is important to remember that even traditional types of testing can be transformed to offer students a chance to think, rather than merely to recall. While tests should not overlook what teachers consider to be essential content, the manner in which that content is approached is important.

Assessment should be considered not only a measure of progress, but also as a continuation and extension of the learning situation for students in assessing their own abilities to think about and apply what has been learned.

CHAPTER SEVEN

Asking Effective Questions Automatically

Teachers who want to improve their questioning skills and apply the ideas in this book need to develop an individual plan of action. When developing their plan, teachers should keep in mind the major goals for questioning: to increase student participation, to raise their levels of thinking, to teach students that the value of facts lies in their application, and to establish how learning relates to students' lives. To accomplish these goals, teachers must:

- Set purposes for the learning that will drive the design of questions toward application or higher-level thinking.
- Inform students at the start of the learning segment how the anticipated knowledge and skill outcomes will benefit them academically and personally.
- Prepare the final evaluation at the start of a unit so that it gives focus to the questioning strategies.
- Inform the students of the method of evaluation so they can direct their studying strategies.
- Provide a variety of opportunities for the students to be actively involved in their learning.

The action plan should be a long-range plan; it should address what the teacher wants to see in two or three years as a result of improved questioning. Thus changes should be made incrementally, rather than trying to do too much at one time. Teachers should use first the ideas and activities with which they feel most comfortable. Other proposed changes should be prioritized, and the selected strategies and activities should be placed on a timeline.

Teachers need to conduct a personal debriefing after each step, keeping notes on the degree to which a strategy worked and indicating any changes to be made the next time it is used. These notes should be reviewed the next time the strategy is used.

In addition to keeping personal notes, the teacher also might choose to ask another teacher or administrator to observe and provide feedback on a new strategy or activity. The students also may be asked to give comments about how they felt about being involved in the learning.

The next step is to become aware of and to eliminate any idiosyncrasies that deter student participation. Examples of such idiosyncrasies were listed in Chapter 2.

Designing Instruction

There are four major activities in which teachers engage that recur during the school year and that affect the design of questioning strategies. These are: 1) implementing a written curriculum and planning instruction, 2) beginning new units of work, 3) making assignments, and 4) making assessments. These recurring activities offer chances for new beginnings and, therefore, recurring opportunities to lend variety to the teaching and learning process. They also provide opportunities for repeating strategies in order to improve them.

Implementing the Curriculum. In most cases, the teacher's lessons are based on the curriculum and text chosen by the district. There also may be state mandates that the teacher must meet; and in the next few years, all of the national discipline committees will have published their ideas of what should be taught. While these might be seen as constraints, the effective teacher will go beyond them. Thus the first task is to examine the content of those sources in order to answer the following questions:

- What were the original questions, concerns, issues, or problems that led to the development of this material? What are the reasons for the study of the discipline, regardless of the content involved?
- What are the major learning outcomes for students who interact with the content?
- What does the content contain that can be transformed into opportunities for students to practice and develop thinking skills?
- What kinds of application activities can be designed for the required content?
- How can the content be related to the students' lives and be made more meaningful to them?

All of the above sources approach instruction from the standpoint of what students should learn. The teacher also should ask, "What will I learn, both about myself and about and from my students?" That focus will help the teacher design questions that both meet the district requirements and involve the students.

Beginning a Unit of Work. There are many ways to begin a unit of work that lend themselves to the design of questions that call for higher-level thinking. One of the easier alternatives is to use one or a combination of the Big Four questions described in Chapter Three. This strategy requires little preparation but is very productive for the students, because what each student knows or wants to know will be known by the other students. Their responses will help the teacher in planning the unit. Asking the Big Four questions should precede the unit by a few days in the primary grades to two or three weeks in the intermediate grades.

Some other ways to begin a unit that will involve the students include:

1. Use evocative and provocative questions or statements for student reaction.
2. Set up a debate.

3. Set up role-playing situations.
4. Use the one-to-five discussion method.

These and other ways to initiate a unit are described in Chapters Three and Four. The teacher should keep a list of various strategies for starting a unit and should add to that list whenever possible.

Teachers should treat these strategies as experiments and test them to see how they compare to other strategies. An elementary teacher can try different strategies with the same group of students in different subject areas to determine the effects of each. Departmentalized and secondary teachers can take advantage of teaching two sections of the same grade and subject by trying different start-up methods to compare their effectiveness.

Making Assignments. When preparing oral or written assignments, the teacher should include three sections: 1) teacher and student questions, for which the answers appear in the source material; 2) questions that require thinking or application; and 3) questions that rely on the results of student experiences and beliefs. The proportion of each type of question will convey a message to the students about what levels of learning are important.

As the year progresses, the proportion of students' questions used in planning each unit should increase, and the proportion of questions from the teacher should decrease. While it probably should not reach the point where the study is based solely on the students' questions, it is important that they feel greater autonomy over their learning. Eventually, the students will be better prepared to ask their own questions when planning individual and personal projects.

Involving the students in questioning at the beginning of a unit often results in questions that require going to resources other than the basic text. That shows students that one text does not have all the answers. To heighten student interest in questioning, the teacher might honor the best question of the week with a wall display in the classroom.

Making Assessments. While assessment is the last of the major recurring actions in the instructional process, the method of evaluation and the questions for the actual test should be decided at the start of each new unit. The items on the test will guide the questioning strategies to be used during the unit.

Preparing the evaluation instrument before the unit begins does not mean that other important ideas that arise during the implementation of the unit cannot be added to the test. However, it will prevent the instruction from straying too far from the intended objectives and learning outcomes.

Working with Students

The success of any change depends on the students as well as on the teacher. There are several strategies that will help the teacher motivate students and lead them to higher-level thinking.

Goal Setting. Asking students to set goals for their learning causes the students to be aware that they have some responsibility for their own learning. It helps them focus their thoughts on what they will do in addition to the objectives and outcomes of the teacher. Also, the students' goals can be used as resources in planning the unit.

Teacher Prompts. The teacher can write a series of questions on index cards to use as prompts for the students. These prompts should be generic questions that ask the students to engage in higher-level thinking. By writing down the various options for a prompt, the teacher will be prepared for the possible student responses and can keep the thinking and discussion moving. With practice, these written prompts will become internalized and will no longer be needed. Some sample prompts include:

- Accept the answer.
- Ask for elaboration.
- Ask for justification or support.
- Ask for clarification.
- Ask for consequences of the response.
- Use active listening.
- Give my own views and experience.

- Give a counter-example.
- Set up a "What if?" situation.
- Play devil's advocate.
- Use deliberate silence (waiting time).
- Show interest in the response.
- Turn to other students for reaction.
- Ask another question.

Prompts can be prepared that promote specific categories of thinking, such as creativity, problem solving, issue resolution, decision making, critiquing, analyzing, or any combination of these strategies. Prompts may be prepared to outline the sequence of a strategy that is aimed at helping students achieve a particular objective.

An added benefit to preparing these prompts is that they also can be given to the students, either as prompt cards or as a classroom display poster.

Student Responsibilities. Teachers should set a few rules for responses so that students will not feel challenged when they are asked for additional information. For example, students should be prepared to support their responses and should provide detailed, rather than general, answers. Students also should speak loudly enough for the entire class to hear.

To increase the possibility that students will contribute, it is a good strategy to ask them to write some responses or questions before the unit begins. Beginning a unit by asking students to write a few thoughts about what they know, think they know, or want to know will allow teachers to call on the student who otherwise might not answer.

Classroom Arrangement. Another positive step is to arrange the class so that students can maintain eye contact. This takes the focus away from the teacher and encourages them to interact.

When the questions are open-ended, students should be given an opportunity to test their ideas and responses in the safety of a small group before presenting them to the entire class. This provides students with a chance to get feedback from their peers about their ideas, opinions, beliefs, and applications. This small-group interaction also may expose them to other ideas, sharpen their thinking, or cause them to rethink their responses because of new or contradicting information. This practice encourages the typically reluctant student to respond.

Conclusion

Planning any new learning sets the stage for the quality of the teaching and learning that will follow. Each teacher must determine how much and how fast the transition to improved questioning will occur. Establishing a long-range plan will make the process manageable and reduce stress.

Teachers must pay attention to both their own and students' roles, methods of preparation, and involvement. Their questions must make students feel that they are a part of the decision on what is to be learned, how it is to be learned, and how they will be evaluated. Improving student participation and stimulating higher-level thinking about and application of the content cannot simply be imposed by a teacher without that type of involvement from students.

Teachers are in control of many of the instructional options that involve learning and decisions about questioning. Creating a humane, unhurried classroom atmosphere that is receptive to students' points of view and questions not only will be conducive to higher levels of student participation, but also will allow the teacher to be a learner as well.

Well-designed questions can bring excitement and interest to any classroom. Drawing on students' ideas enriches learning. And preparing appropriate responses to students' answers can deepen learning. The challenge of enriching not only the content of learning but also the students' engagement in that learning is a powerful challenge for all teachers.

APPENDICES

APPENDIX 1

What Makes a Good Question?

Following is a checklist of characteristics that tend to make questions elicit higher-order thinking.

The question . . .

- ☐ Has no one "right" answer.
- ☐ Is open-ended.
- ☐ Calls for reflection.
- ☐ Can be answered based on students' knowledge.
- ☐ Is interesting to students.
- ☐ Motivates or stimulates thinking.
- ☐ Demonstrates a search for understanding.
- ☐ Allows for individual input based on prior knowledge.
- ☐ Provokes more questions.
- ☐ Promotes discussion.
- ☐ Raises students' curiosity.
- ☐ Challenges preconceptions.

Why Test?

Following is a short list of statements. Teachers should be able to complete one or more of these statements as they determine their purpose(s) for testing:

This test will . . .

       teach students to _____.

       cause students to learn _____.

       enable students to show _____.

       cause students to practice _____.

Tips for Preparing Written Tests

Following are eight tips to ensure that the test form facilitates, rather than impedes, higher-order responses.

1. Check carefully to eliminate grammar and spelling errors.

2. Type or use a word processor; do not hand-write the test.

3. Use capitals and lowercase, not just capitals.

4. Check all questions for accuracy.

5. Avoid merely repeating questions asked in class.

6. Avoid giving away the answer to one question in another question.

7. If possible, keep the test questions in one section on the same page; start a new section on a new page.

8. Use standard question formats and do not mix formats randomly — that is, put true-false questions together in a section and multiple-choice questions in another section if you plan to use both formats.

Test-Taking Strategies for Students

Following are tips that will help students do their best on tests.

Before the test:

- Understand the homework before you leave class.
- Do your homework.
- Make a study schedule and stick to it.
- Ask your teacher for additional help if you need it.
- Find out what kind of test will be given and any special test rules.
- Don't skip a meal before the test; it's harder to think on an empty stomach.

During the test:

- Read all directions carefully.
- Follow directions.
- If you can choose among answers, read all of the possible choices first; then choose.
- Skip difficult questions and come back to them later.
- Answer as many questions as possible.
- When you finish, check your work.
- Think positive!

Evaluating Student Responses

Many factors can affect how students respond to questions. Some points worth considering are highlighted below:

Depth of prior knowledge

How much time was spent on prior learning?
Was the approach a survey or intensive study?
Was the textbook the sole or main source of information?

Recency of learning

When was the topic studied? For how long?
To what extent was the student involved in studying the topic?

Interest or motivation

How much interest did the student show in the topic?
Did the student go beyond the required amount of study?
Has the student demonstrated independent study?

Ability

What is a reasonable level of expectation for the student?

Attention

Does the student show a willingness to learn?

Classroom Observation

Following is a two-part classroom observation protocol, which is designed to assist an observer in recording impressions and assessing the questioning strategies used during the observation period.

Course _____ Grade _____

Teacher _____

Date and time of observation _____

What the Teacher Did

1. Did the following take place?
   - ☐ The teacher explained the objective(s) of the lesson, unit, etc.
   - ☐ The teacher involved students in setting goals for the lesson.
   - ☐ The teacher gave the students a syllabus.
   - ☐ The teacher surveyed students to ascertain their prior knowledge.
   - ☐ The teacher elicited questions from students prior to beginning the lesson.

2. Tally the number of questions asked by the teacher that called for:

   Concrete, factual, or "right" answers _____

   Teacher elaboration or explanation _____

   Student elaboration or explanation _____

3. Estimate the percentage of class time that the teacher used for:

Lecture _____

Elaboration/explanation of questions _____

4. If there were pencil-and-paper activities, did they call for:
   - ☐ Factual answers
   - ☐ Thinking skills
   - ☐ Essay writing
   - ☐ Other types of answers (describe) _____

5. How were students arranged?
   - ☐ Seats in rows
   - ☐ Small groups
   - ☐ Other (describe) _____

6. How was the class presentation organized?
   - ☐ Mainly teacher lecture
   - ☐ Some teacher lecture and some question-and-answer
   - ☐ Mainly question-and-answer
   - ☐ Mainly class or small-group discussion
   - ☐ Other (describe) _____

7. What percentage of talk in class was student-to-student?

   _____

8. How many times did the teacher ask students to elaborate, defend, or explain an answer?_____

9. Did the teacher or students summarize the class work?

   _____

10. Was an assignment made for the next class session? _____

11. If the teacher gave an assignment, what was it?

    _____

12. Did the teacher announce the topic for the next day?

    _____

13. To what extent did the teacher:

repeat questions?	seldom	sometimes	often
repeat student answers?	seldom	sometimes	often
answer his or her own questions?	seldom	sometimes	often
pause for 5 or more seconds after asking a question?	seldom	sometimes	often
pause for 5 or more seconds after receiving a student answer?	seldom	sometimes	often

What the Students Did

1. How many students were in the class? _____

2. How many students actively participated (answered, discussed, etc.)? _____

3. If one or two students are most vocal, tally the number of times they respond.

   _____

   _____

4. How many student-generated questions:
   ask for factual answers? _____
   ask for teacher explanations? _____
   ask for the teacher to repeat something? _____
   ask for permission? _____
   other (explain) _____

5. Rank the top five roles assumed by students in the class:
   _____ Listening
   _____ Answering factual questions
   _____ Participating in small-group discussion
   _____ Participating in whole-group discussion
   _____ Using notes to answer questions
   _____ Referring to a text or other source of information
   _____ Engaging in an activity
   _____ Reading silently with direction (that is, assigned reading)

_____ Reading silently without direction (that is, personal
        or free reading)
_____ Reading aloud
_____ Completing a worksheet
_____ Reviewing a worksheet or homework assignment
_____ Other (describe) _____

6. How many students appeared to be disengaged or not paying
   attention? _____

7. Were students able to hear other students' answers?

                              seldom   sometimes   often

General Observations

Record statements or questions under the following categories:
   Misinformation given by the teacher or students.
   Misperceptions that should be explored in future classes.
   Indications of bias or prejudice that should be examined.
   Indications of limited or poor-quality thinking.
   Misspellings in written material (on the board or on paper).
   Statements that require clarification, explanation, or justifica-
      tion.

APPENDIX 7

Analyzing the Classroom Observation

Following are some notes that may be helpful in analyzing the observations. The notes are keyed to the item numbers of the observation protocol.

What the Teacher Did

1. All of the practices listed are positive. Students benefit from knowing what they are expected to learn and how they will go about it. Teachers can better structure lessons effectively if they survey students to find out what they already know and what questions they have at the outset.

2. Higher-order thinking most often takes place when it is the student who responds to a question by elaborating or explaining his or her thinking. "Right" answers elicit only memory responses, and teacher elaboration often diminishes student input.

3. If the percentages here are high, then students are passive. The goal should be to involve students *actively* as much as possible.

4. Pencil-and-paper activities that require authentic student writing are most likely to generate higher-order thinking.

5. Although students can be active even while seated in traditional rows of desks, small groups tend to facilitate more active engagement of all students.

6. This list is somewhat progressive, from low student involvement ("mainly teacher lecture") to high involvement. The more involved that students are, the better.

7. In general, student discussion should be encouraged. But it also should be class-centered and not merely chatter.

8. Teachers who ask students to elaborate, defend, or explain answers are eliciting higher-order thinking. The more often this happens, the greater the learning.

9. A summary, preferably by students, usually helps to pull a lesson together and to set the stage for the next day's work or that day's homework.

10, 11, 12. While written homework is not absolutely necessary, students should not leave class without something to think about, if only what to anticipate the next day.

13. These are actions simply to be alert to. If a teacher has to repeat questions, he or she should consider whether the questions may be too complex — or perhaps the wait time is too short. Pausing for 5 or more seconds after a question or an answer can bring forth additional student responses.

What the Students Did

1, 2, 3. The answers here are baseline demographics that help to indicate the extent of active student participation.

4. High numbers of responses to these items indicate lower-level questioning on the part of students.

5. Consider: Are the five top roles mainly active or passive? The more active students are, in general the more they are learning.

6, 7. These questions can help gauge whether (and possibly why) some students are not involved in active learning.

General Observations

This record is designed to help the teacher discern problem areas that should be corrected, whether they are minor (such as misspelled words on the board or a handout) or fairly significant (such as misstatements of information).

RESOURCES

Bateman, Walter L. *Open to Questioning: The Art of Teaching and Learning by Inquiry*. San Francisco: Jossey-Bass, 1990.

Beyer, Barry K. *Practical Strategies for the Teaching of Thinking*. Boston: Allyn and Bacon, 1987.

Blackey, Robert. "Bull's-Eye: A Teachers' Guide for Developing Student Skill in Responding to Essay Questions." *Social Education* 52, no. 10 (1988): 464-66.

Bloom, Benjamin S., ed. *Taxonomy of Educational Objectives: The Classification of Educational Goals: Handbook 1: Cognitive Domain*. New York: David McKay, 1956.

Brown, Neil M., and Keeley, Stuart M. *Asking the Right Questions: A Guide to Critical Thinking*. 2nd ed. Englewood Cliffs, N.J.: Prentice-Hall, 1986.

Bruner, J. *Toward a Theory of Instruction*. Cambridge, Mass.: Belknap Press, 1966.

Chuska, Kenneth R. *Fourteen Connections, or How to Study Everything*. Fastback 502. Bloomington, Ind.: Phi Delta Kappa Educational Foundation, 2002.

Chuska, Kenneth R. *Teaching the Process of Thinking, K-12*. Fastback 244. Bloomington, Ind.: Phi Delta Kappa Educational Foundation, 1986.

Cotton, Kathleen. "Classroom Questioning." *School Improvement Research Series III*. Northwest Regional Educational Laboratory, 1989. www.nwrel.org/scpd/sirs/3/cu5.html.

Dillon, J.T. *Questioning and Teaching*. New York: Teachers College Press, 1988.

Eberle, Robert F. *SCAMPER: Games for Imagination Development*. Buffalo: D.O.K. Publishers, 1971.

Gordon, Thomas. *T.E.T.: Teacher Effectiveness Training*. New York: Peter H. Wyden, 1974.

Hudgins, Bryce B. *Learning and Thinking: A Primer for Teachers*. Itasca, Ill.: F.E. Peacock, 1977.

Hunkins, Francis P. *Involving Students in Questioning.* Boston: Allyn and Bacon, 1976.

Junior Great Books. *An Introduction to Inquiry.* 3rd ed. Chicago: Great Books Foundation, 1992.

Marzano, Robert J.; Pickering, Debra; and McTighe, Jay. *Assessing Student Outcomes: Performance Assessment Using the Dimensions of Learning.* Alexandria, Va.: Association for Supervision and Curriculum Development, 1993.

Marzano, Robert J., et al. *Dimensions of Thinking: A Framework for Curriculum and Instruction.* Alexandria, Va.: Association for Supervision and Curriculum Development, 1988.

National Commission on Excellence in Education. *A Nation at Risk: The Imperative for Educational Reform.* Washington, D.C.: U.S. Department of Education, 1983.

Osborn, Alex F. *Applied Imagination.* 3rd ed. rev. New York: Charles Scribner's Sons, 1963.

Palincsar, A.S., and Brown, A.L. "Reciprocal Teaching of Comprehension-Fostering and Comprehension-Monitoring Activities." *Cognition and Instruction* 1 (1985): 117-75.

Rowe, Mary Budd. "Wait-Time and Rewards as Instruction Variables: Their Influence on Language, Logic and Fate Control: Part 1: Wait-Time." *Journal of Research in Science Teaching* 11, no. 2 (1974): 81-84.

Russell, David H. *Children's Thinking.* Waltham, Mass.: Blaisdell, 1956.

Sanders, Norris M. *Classroom Questions: What Kinds?* New York: Harper & Row, 1966.

Secretary's Commission on Achieving Necessary Skills. *Learning a Living: A Blueprint for High Performance: A SCANS Report for America 2000.* Washington, D.C.: U.S. Department of Education, 1992.

Taba, Hilda. *Teaching Strategies and Cognitive Functioning in Elementary School Children.* Cooperative Research Project No. 2404. San Francisco: San Francisco State University, 1966.

Torrance, E.P., and Myers, R.E. *Creative Learning and Teaching.* New York: Dodd, Mead, 1970.

Upton, Albert. *A Design for Teaching.* Palo Alto, Calif.: Pacific Books, 1961.

ABOUT THE AUTHOR

Kenneth R. Chuska is an education consultant. He has taught in the Pittsburgh Public Schools and served in administrative positions in the Peters Township School District near Pittsburgh. Most recently he was program administrator for the gifted and talented and coordinator of curriculum development for the handicapped at the Allegheny Intermediate Unit, a regional public school service agency in the Pittsburgh, Pennsylvania area. He has been an elementary and secondary teacher, a principal, an elementary supervisor, and a K-12 curriculum coordinator.

Chuska received his A.B. degree in secondary English and the social sciences and his M.Ed. in elementary education and administration from the University of Pittsburgh. His doctoral dissertation at the same institution was a study of the provisions for the gifted in the elementary schools of Pennsylvania.

He has taught courses in curriculum, diagnostic teaching, education of the gifted, and thinking skills at Pennsylvania State University. He has conducted workshops on thinking for several state departments of education, Phi Delta Kappa International, and other organizations.

Chuska has served on task forces for the Association for Supervision and Curriculum Development, the National Institute of Education, and the Pennsylvania Department of Education. His articles have appeared in the Pennsylvania Department of Education's *Thinking Newsletter* and other professional publications. He also is the author of fastbacks 244 *Teaching the Process of Thinking, K-12* and 502 *Fourteen Connections, or How to Study Everything*, published by the Phi Delta Kappa Educational Foundation, and *Gifted Learners, K-12: A Practical Guide to Effective Curriculum and Teaching*, published by the National Educational Service.

WGRL-HQ NONFIC
31057100077372
371.37 CHUSK
Chuska, Kenneth R.
Improving classroom questions